SPIRIT AFLAME

Luis Palau's Mission to London

SPIRIT AFLAME

Luis Palau's Mission to London

by

Susan Holton
and
David L. Jones

HODDER AND STOUGHTON
LONDON SYDNEY AUCKLAND TORONTO

British Library Cataloguing in Publication Data

Holton, Susan
Spirit aflame
1. Evangelistic work – England
I. Title   II. Jones, David
269'.2'0942   BV3777.G7

ISBN 0 340 37401 2

CONTENTS

FOREWORD

It is hard to imagine a greater privilege than serving as Executive Director of the Luis Palau Mission to London. Exhilaration and exhaustion went hand in hand as we reached out with the good news of Jesus Christ to the capital.

Spirit Aflame chronicles the exploits of a faithful band of men and women who set out to achieve the impossible. Do not expect this book to tell the full story. There are four good reasons why it cannot.

Firstly, the story is just too big. The sheer scale of the enterprise and the tens of thousands that it touched demand many more words than there will ever be space available.

Secondly, much of the story has yet to unfold. For each person who responded publicly there are countless others who did so privately. And there are the friends and families of those who responded who now have made their own commitment to Christ as the domino effect goes into operation.

Then there is the fact that *Spirit Aflame* does not set out to be a 'warts and all' record of history. Mission to London was run by a dedicated team of very human people, all as capable of making mistakes as anyone else. This book sets out to be a testimony to what God did through fallible people, not what his people failed to do.

Finally, we should recognise that those who have written *Spirit Aflame* have a close association with the Luis Palau Evangelistic Team. This has inhibited them from handing out the accolades that their colleagues so richly deserve.

So it should be put on record that each member of the Luis Palau Team proved to be displaying a gentle and humble spirit, and a real servant attitude. They were a great gift to London.

In terms of numbers, the number of adults making a first-time commitment to Christ through the Mission is the equivalent of starting eighty-two new churches each with 114 members. This book tells the story honestly, truthfully and powerfully. Read it – and give God all the credit.

PETER MEADOWS
20 February, 1985

PREFACE

'Let this be written for a future generation, that a people not yet created may praise the Lord' (Psalm 102:18).

That is a command from Holy Scripture. We are to write down not so much what we have done, but what the Lord has done.

I believe this book recounts what the Lord has done in Greater London in this generation as the end of the twentieth century draws ever closer. This book outlines the backdrop, analyses some of the forces that have shaped London today, and then shares the great things that God has done through a united evangelistic outreach called Mission to London.

I believe that people not yet born will praise Him when they read how God touched the great metropolis of London at a time of unprecedented secularism and minimal biblical knowledge.

Throughout British history Christians from John Wesley to George Whitefield to Dwight L. Moody to Billy Graham have recorded God's victories. As we read these exciting accounts, our hearts are thrilled, and we realise that if God could move so tremendously in Britain years ago, He can do it today as He works through us.

I believe God will be glorified by this record of what He has done in London in the 1980s. In 1739 George Whitefield, the great British evangelist, said: 'I see more and more the benefit of leaving written testimonies behind us . . . They not only profit the present, but will also edify the future age.'[1] Generations yet to come will be inspired and motivated by this new account of God transforming lives through the preaching of the Gospel.

My prayer is that this book shall bring all the glory and honour to whom it truly belongs – our Lord and Saviour Jesus Christ. Certainly no participant in Mission to London wishes to take any credit or glory himself. We made many mistakes, we missed some unusual opportunities, and perhaps twelve weeks of preaching the Gospel were not enough. But the Lord chose to use us as we joined hands with London churches so that the name of Jesus was lifted up to the millions in this international city.

We are thrilled as we continue to hear stories of transformed lives. The promise of 2 Corinthians 5:17 – 'If anyone is in Christ, he is a new creation; the old has gone, the new has come!' – was fulfilled thousands of times in London. During the mission the educated and privileged, as well as the poor and hungry, were converted by Christ. Now these people from all classes and ethnic backgrounds are singing their praises to God.

I am also thrilled that many churches involved in the mission have reported tremendous growth in attendance. A few have reported doubled and even tripled attendances.

I shall never forget the joyful singing and praising of God we heard in London – a unique feature of British evangelical life in the 1970s and 1980s. Seeing English boys, girls, men and women worshipping Jesus Christ and centring their thoughts on God our Father is an unforgettable picture in my mind.

One Saturday morning during the mission more than eighteen thousand children and counsellors filled Queen's Park Rangers stadium for the Rainbow Special. This outstanding children's ministry and the amazing number of children who gave their lives to Christ is a challenge for the future. The mandate is clear: the children of London *can* be reached by the Good News of a loving Saviour. One of my prayers is that this book will stir many to devote themselves to reach the children and young people of London for Christ.

In this book you will also read about how the last week of June 1984 marked a historic pinnacle in world evangelism. Through an international radio and television strategy called Commonwealth 84, the mission's Gospel messages pen-

etrated more than fifty English-speaking nations, many of
them in the Third World. Commonwealth 84 was well worth
the tremendous investment of effort, time, personnel and
finances. Months after the mission ended we were still
receiving exciting letters from all over the globe which tell
how the Commonwealth 84 messages changed hearts and
lives for Jesus Christ.

I am also thrilled that we were ministering in Britain at the
same time that our esteemed brother, Dr Billy Graham, was
proclaiming the Gospel in six British cities. His team's
Mission England saw an even greater harvest of souls than we
did. More than one million personally attended Dr Graham's
meetings, and an incredible 96,982 people – 9.4 per cent of
the audience – registered public Christian commitments.

To minister in Britain at the same time as Dr Graham
was a historic time for me personally. As a teenager in Argentina I read about Dr Graham's 1954 London campaign at
Harringay Arena and dreamed great dreams of someday
proclaiming the Gospel in London. But never did I imagine
that I would have the honour of ministering in Britain
simultaneously with Dr Graham. During Mission to London
I was pleased to speak at one of his Mission England meetings, and I was honoured when he addressed the Mission
to London crowd at QPR stadium. His stirring message
and encouragement were extremely welcome on one of the
coldest and wettest nights of the mission.

Mission to London will be remembered as a joyful, unified
crusade by those who attended. At the end, the team members, the committees and thousands of volunteers were
physically exhausted. Yet night after night the choir sang
joyfully, the crowd listened intently, and multitudes came
forward to confess Jesus Christ as their Saviour and Lord.
That was the greatest climax and most God-glorifying aspect
of the entire crusade. That some twenty-eight thousand
people from a cautious and pragmatic population like London's should publicly confess Christ is one of the greatest
demonstrations of the power of God working in Britain in this
generation.

Our prayer is that the fire lit during Billy Graham's

Mission England and our own Mission to London will be
fanned into a flame of revival. We will continue to pray that
before the year 2000 an even mightier harvest will be brought
into Jesus Christ's Church in Britain. We pray that the
spiritual flame we ignited will spill into continental Europe,
where the needs are even greater.

I want to add the words of that old hymn – words that
deserve to be sung again: 'To God be the glory! Great things
He has done.' We commend this book to the glory of God by
repeating the words of the psalmist: 'Let this be written for a
future generation, that a people not yet created may praise
the Lord.'

May you, too, praise Him as you read this thrilling story.

                                        LUIS PALAU

SECTION ONE

SETTING THE STAGE
FOR THE MISSION

Chapter 1

FANNING REVIVAL FLAMES

London, 14 July 1984. On this rainy, cool night more than twenty-three thousand people jam the stands and spill on to the pitch at Queen's Park Rangers' stadium. They aren't the same rowdy football crowd QPR usually attracts. No football match is scheduled for tonight.

This is *another* QPR, home of the Luis Palau Mission to London. The slogan here for the past six weeks has been 'Let the whole of London hear the voice of God'. Instead of goals and penalties, progress has been measured by attendance and spiritual decisions.

Since the end of May, 293,000 people have passed through the turnstiles at QPR to attend the mission. Some have come from curiosity to hear this Argentine evangelist. Others have come as a favour to a family member or friend. Still others have come on a whim, knowing only that they don't want to miss this event being talked about all over London.

Tonight coaches, trains and the underground have brought passengers from Brixton, Clapham, Acton, Islington, Barnet, Ealing, Walthamstow and Hounslow; from Kent, Surrey, Sussex, Essex and Berkshire; and even from Scotland, Wales, Finland, Canada, the Middle East and South America. Whatever their background, they're keenly aware that they are witnessing the climax of a historic mission.

Mission to London was memorable in many ways. Among them:

★ More than fifteen thousand London Christians mobilised and trained to reach their city for Christ.

★ The cooperation of more than seventeen hundred

London churches in a truly interdenominational endeavour.

*The first time so many religious broadcasters united to carry the Gospel to most of the English-speaking world.

*The most media coverage – most of it favourable – Palau had ever received during a crusade.

*A publicity campaign that succeeded in making almost everyone in London aware of the Mission to London.

*The highest percentage of enquirers Palau had witnessed in his nine years of ministry in Britain.

*So many new converts being incorporated into churches that many churches reported 25 per cent increases in the size of their congregations, and some churches even doubled in size!

Sheila Walsh, a guest musician at QPR, remarked: 'God is doing something here. I have a feeling that at the moment we are seeing things in Britain that are changing the face of history. We're really going to see great things happen.'

The Rev. Rob Frost, a Methodist minister, agreed. Mentioning Britain's dismal years of church decline, Frost said: 'Mission to London has brought results, but the main impact won't be felt for ten, twenty or thirty years when the young people who have given their lives to Jesus Christ during the mission become ministers and church leaders with a real love for the Lord and a desire to serve Him.'

Reports of thousands of changed lives testify that the impact of Mission to London is just beginning.

Early in the second phase of the two-phased Mission to London, an entire family from Colombia, South America, came to Christ at QPR stadium.

The leader of a punk rock group found new life in Christ there.

A professional photographer hired to photograph Mission to London opened his heart to Christ at a mission women's meeting. Later he brought his wife, and she also received Christ.

A minicab driver from All Saints' Church, Brixton Hill, picked up a depressed passenger, shared the Gospel with her, invited her to come with his family, and watched her give her life to Christ at the stadium.

A woman hired a minibus to bring eighteen young people to hear the Gospel. At the invitation, all eighteen went forward and gave their lives to Christ.

A fifteen-year-old wrote: 'I had to write this letter as I have just witnessed a miracle. Last night my friend and I took twelve of our non-Christian friends to QPR. We had prayed that the message would sink in. You can imagine our joy when all of them gave their lives to Christ.'

Another letter reads: 'My Christian friends had been trying to lead me to Christ for a year, but I held out. After hearing you at QPR I realised that I had to go one way or the other, so I chose the right way.'

Another letter: 'The first time I came to QPR I felt that God was calling me, but I was afraid. The second time I felt it again, and I accepted your invitation to ask Christ into my life. On my third visit I brought a friend, and she committed her life to Christ. Since becoming a Christian I am a new person.'

Hundreds of the 23,000 jammed into QPR on this final night of the mission would choose to follow Christ and would experience similar transformations in the days ahead.

David Pickford, Mission to London chairman, presented an ornamental clock to Palau as an expression of the gratitude of London's Christians. Alluding to Shakespeare, Pickford told Palau: 'You came to London, you saw our need, and you conquered our hearts by your love, your witness and your ministry.'

Making his third appearance at QPR, musician Cliff Richard spoke of Britain's renewed interest in Christianity: 'In the last five years people have begun asking questions to find out what Christians have to offer, and to see if Christianity is valid for them. Both Luis Palau and Billy Graham have said they've noticed an increasing responsiveness to the preaching of the Gospel in Britain.'

Peter Meadows, executive director of Mission to London, said the ten-month campaign was the largest Christian event in London since Billy Graham's London crusade in the 1960s. 'I don't believe there has been a time in the last twenty

years when the churches have had such a golden opportunity
for real revival to take place.'

Palau concluded his fortieth and last night of preaching
with these words: 'Jesus Christ, the Son of God, is as alive
tonight at QPR as he was two thousand years ago in Palestine.
He loves you. He died on the cross for our sins – yours and
mine. He wants to come into your life, but you must invite
Him to come in.

'I pray that hundreds and even thousands of you will open
your hearts to the Lord Jesus. In the Bible Jesus says, "I
stand at the door and knock. If anyone hears my voice and
opens the door, I will come in and eat with him, and he with
me" (Revelation 3:20).

'It's your decision. In St Paul's Cathedral is a painting of
Jesus holding a lamp and knocking on a door. Only you can
open the door of your heart to Jesus Christ. He is knocking on
your door. Will you let Him in? You must make the decision.

'This is your moment of decision. In a moment we're going
to stand for prayer. All of you who want to know the peace of
Christ, open your heart to the Lord Jesus.

'You'll never forget 14 July 1984. You'll never forget that
on a cool, rainy night God entered your life. He will begin to
change you, control you, and fill you with His peace. Those
of you who want to know that peace with God, and that inner
peace that comes from the Holy Spirit, pray with us to the
living Christ. I hope that not one of you will walk away
without making this important decision.'

Earlier in the evening Palau had told the crowd, 'I believe
this will be among the greatest nights in years in London in
terms of the number of people professing Christ.'

He was right. As the choir sang the invitation hymn 'Jesus
I Come' for the last time, nearly one thousand people
streamed on to the pitch to publicly announce their faith in
Christ.

All told, some twenty-eight thousand people made public
decisions for Christ during the two phases of Mission to
London – in September and October 1983 and in June and
July 1984. Many more of the 500,000 who attended the
mission made decisions privately but never signed commit-

ment cards, as mission leaders learned when letters began arriving from unregistered enquirers.

One such letter addressed to Luis Palau reads: 'When you began appearing on all the tube trains and stations in London inviting me to 'bring my doubts to QPR' I decided to give it a shot. I had plenty of doubts to bring. As I sat and listened, you began to get through to me. I started to get the disturbing feeling that some of what you said might be true.

'I thought about it for several days and then sat down to write you a letter, listing all my arguments as to why I didn't believe in Christ until, halfway through the letter, I realised what I had written wasn't true . . .

'With Mission to London you have awakened something in thousands of people which can only be good for the city. I shall be praying for you as you continue around the world. I came to the final night at QPR as a Christian, and as I sat on the pitch in front of the platform I felt a contentment I've never felt before.

'For the first time in my life I have Someone I can trust and depend upon totally. You introduced me to Jesus, and I thank you from the bottom of my heart.'

The final night saw the conclusion of a chapter in the story of Christianity in London.

The Rev. Gilbert Kirby, chairman of the mission's executive committee, said: 'We have all learned a great deal from Mission to London. But above all, we desire to give glory to God for the wonderful way in which He has worked among us.'

Kirby added: 'Time and time again our feeble faith was rebuked. We are conscious that only eternity will reveal the full story. We recognise the enormity of the task facing the churches as they seek to integrate so many babes into their fellowships.'

But Peter Meadows, executive director of Mission to London, hinted that an even more exciting chapter was just beginning: 'So far as London is concerned, much has been achieved. But we have just begun!'

Chapter 2

BRITAIN'S CHRISTIAN HERITAGE

'Christians everywhere owe a great spiritual debt to England,' said the Rev. Gottfried Osei-Mensah, former executive secretary for the Lausanne Committee for World Evangelization. He noted that many of the Church's revivals, awakenings and mission movements began in England.[1]

The United Kingdom has also given birth to many historic denominations: Episcopalians, Methodists, Baptists, Presbyterians, Brethren, Congregationalists, Salvation Army and Quakers, as well as the Elim and Apostolic Pentecostal churches and the Church of Christ. And Britain has produced some of history's most famous Christian workers: John Wesley, George Whitefield, William Carey, Hudson Taylor and William Booth.

Today, immorality and spiritual decay are widespread in Britain but these problems are not unique to the 20th century. The country suffered similar problems in the early eighteenth century prior to her Great Awakening. Crimes were committed so frequently in London that one source says: 'London almost ceased to be a civilised town . . . The nation was almost drowned in liquor.'[2]

Another source says that in 1749 'every sixth house in London was a public house. Signs invited the poor to get drunk for a penny, dead-drunk for two-pence, and have straw on which to lie and recover free. Drunkenness was a national vice.'[3]

The church lost its power.

WHITEFIELD AND WESLEY

The preaching of three young Methodists from Oxford –
John and Charles Wesley and George Whitefield – was the
spark that ignited Britain's Great Awakening. One historian
explained, 'There never was less religious feeling, either
within the Establishment or without, than when Wesley
blew his trumpet, and awakened those who slept.'[4]

As a student at Oxford University, George Whitefield
joined the Methodist group, or the Holy Club, led by John
Wesley. In 1738, Whitefield went to America and challenged
the popular doctrine that water baptism alone was needed for
salvation. Upon returning to Britain, Whitefield found his
preaching much in demand among the people, but English
churches had closed their doors to him. Whitefield did the
unthinkable by preaching in the open air to a mass of coal
miners at Kingswood Hill in 1739. In that era in Britain,
preaching was done solely in churches, but Whitefield's
open-air preaching immediately gained popularity with the
masses. At his first sermon, Whitefield spoke to 200, but his
second sermon attracted 2,000, and soon massive crowds
were gathering in open fields to hear him preach.

Whitefield urged John Wesley to join him in open-air
preaching, and although Wesley was at first reluctant to leave
his growing ministry in London, he agreed to join Whitefield
in Bristol. When 3,000 gathered to hear Wesley's first sermon
there, he became a firm believer in open-air preaching, and
began travelling from city to city, speaking to the thousands
who gathered to hear about Jesus Christ.

The church offered an elegant religion to the rich, but
Wesley offered salvation and eternal life to all people, regard-
less of social status, by preaching the then ignored doctrine of
salvation by grace through faith.

After making more than two hundred evangelistic visits to
London, Wesley reflected on the changed spiritual and moral
condition of the city when he said: 'I believe there is no place
but London where we have so many souls devoted to
God.'[5]

He added: 'The fields in every part of England are indeed white for harvest.'[6]

Whitefield, too, travelled throughout Britain, preaching on commons and in fields to the masses who gathered to hear the Gospel.

During Mission to London, Luis Palau preached at some of the same sites where Whitefield spoke during the Great Awakening two and a half centuries earlier. Blackheath was one of them. Whitefield wrote in his journal: 'Preached . . . in the evening to about 20,000 at Blackheath. It rained, but few were driven away by it. God watered us with the dew of His heavenly blessing. Oh that we may all grow in grace in the knowledge of our Lord and Saviour Jesus Christ.'[7]

Crowds continued to grow. At one point, Whitefield preached to an estimated eighty thousand people near Hyde Park Corner. As the evangelical revival continued, thousands more were converted, and Britain's spiritual condition was rejuvenated.

But less than a hundred years later, British ministers were again delivering carefully prepared theological essays, lacking any vital religion or personal relationship with Christ.

Charles Haddon Spurgeon, one of the greatest orators who ever lived, again fired up Britain's churches, especially in London. Born in 1834, Spurgeon preached his first sermon at sixteen, and at twenty was asked to pastor London's New Park Street Chapel. This church, which seated 1,200, had rarely attracted 300 before Spurgeon's arrival, but his sermons soon filled the church to overflowing.

Wrote one biographer: 'Mr Spurgeon's entrance into London was almost like the throwing in of a bombshell . . . London needed a message of vital religion and spiritual life. Spurgeon had the message.'[8]

Attendance at Spurgeon's New Park Street Chapel grew at a tremendous rate, so the twenty-one-year-old pastor moved his congregation into the new 6,000-seat Metropolitan Tabernacle. During Spurgeon's thirty-seven years there the congregation continued to grow, and his sermons were regularly published by London newspapers.

BRITAIN'S GREAT MISSIONARIES

Fortunately for the rest of the world, Britain's revived Christians didn't keep their blessings to themselves. Missionaries from Britain were in the forefront of the first great cross-cultural evangelism efforts in the history of Protestant Christianity.

But the idea of reaching out into foreign countries and cultures with the Gospel was not popular until William Carey founded the Baptist Missionary Society in 1792. Missionaries did exist before Carey, but Carey's was the first modern world missions endeavour undertaken not by ecclesiastical leaders but by laymen. Carey encountered incredible opposition.

In a *Christian Herald* article Luis Palau explained the boredom and doubt Carey encountered when he proposed sending British missionaries to evangelise the world: 'Older Christians told him to give up his preposterous ideas. But in explaining his dreams and plans, Carey wrote: "Expect great things from God. Attempt great things for God." That statement became the creed of the modern missions movement.'[9]

One of those influenced by Carey's fruitful work was Hudson Taylor, who determined at seventeen to be a missionary in China. Taylor sailed for China at the age of twenty-one. Unordained, and having taught himself Chinese, he worked as an independent missionary in China for twelve years until he established the China Inland Mission in 1865. Except for periodic furloughs in England, he served in China until his death in 1905.

China Inland Mission became Overseas Missionary Fellowship (OMF) in the 1950s when the Communist seizure of China ended all foreign missionary activity there. But China's church survived and grew, while OMF became more active in other parts of East Asia. The work Taylor began more than a century ago is still producing fruit.

Taylor's faith in God answering prayer was greatly influenced by a German missionary, George Mueller. While Taylor was pointing the way to Christ to the poor in China,

Mueller was ministering to the poor of Bristol.

Born in Germany in 1805 and educated in theology at the University of Halle, Mueller dedicated himself entirely to the Lord's service when he was twenty. He moved to London where he distributed free Bibles and other Christian literature. He then moved on to the West Country, finally establishing Christian day schools for the poor in Bristol. Mueller's most notable accomplishment was his establishment of several orphanages which by 1875 were lodging, feeding and educating up to two thousand English children at any given time. Believing that God would provide his every need, he refused any salary and depended solely on voluntary contributions.

Many impoverished Londoners were reached through the ministry of William Booth, founder of The Salvation Army. Converted to Christ at the age of fifteen, he immediately began his lifelong work of saving the souls of those living in deep poverty, a work that was the beginning of The Salvation Army.

Before his death in 1912, Booth saw The Salvation Army ministry spread from Britain to twenty-two countries. The fruitful work of The Salvation Army still continues today because of his faithful service.

Another branch of the evangelistic work in nineteenth-century Britain was mass campaigns, much like Palau's Mission to London.

Charles Finney was an American evangelist who campaigned in Britain in the 1850s. When Finney arrived in London, spiritual apathy prevailed in Britain. Finney attacked the spiritual deadness with zeal, preaching in London five nights a week and twice on Sunday for a total of thirty-six weeks.

MOODY'S MISSION TO LONDON

Among the best-known evangelistic crusades in Britain were the original Mission to London campaigns led by American

evangelist Dwight L. Moody. Tens of thousands responded
to the Gospel during 1875 and 1884.

During the four-month Mission to London in 1875,
Moody spoke at 280 meetings with total attendance exceeding 2.5 million. Most of these meetings were in Islington's
Agricultural Hall, which had been adapted to seat 15,000,
although attendance averaged 20,000 nightly.

Moody opened one of these meetings by saying: 'God has
laid it upon the heart of the world to pray for London. It must
be that God has something good in store for London; the Son
of man is coming to London to seek and to save that which
was lost . . . Let us praise Him for what He is going to do in
London.'[10]

In 1884 Moody returned to London for an eight-month
campaign in various locations throughout London. He
addressed an average of 9,000 per day, and an average of
25,000 on Sundays, with an estimated total audience of 2·2
million.

Although thousands were converted during Moody's
London campaigns, many opposed his work, especially the
London press, which called Moody's accent 'broadly vulgar
and American' and his teaching 'wild, baseless and uncer-
tain'. *The Morning Advertiser* reported about one of Moody's
meetings: 'There must have been thousands in that crowd of
uplifted faces who looked with horror and shame on the
illiterate preacher making little better than a travesty of all
they held sacred.'[11]

Moody replied that Christians must expect opposition. 'If
you think a great work is to be done here without opposition
you will be greatly mistaken,' he said.[12]

Palau's Mission to London in 1983 and 1984 was similar to
D. L. Moody's London missions. Both evangelists preached
straight from the Bible, relating God's Word to their audiences in direct, simple language. Both Moody and Palau
addressed many groups such as businessmen and children
during the day in addition to the nightly general meetings.
Both campaigns also incorporated associate evangelists
speaking to additional meetings, large choirs to minister in
music, prayer meetings before each service, and an enquiry

area filled with counsellors to assist those who responded to the Gospel during the meetings. Both Moody and Palau addressed campaign meetings at Clapham Common and in Fairfield Halls in Croydon.

In 1901 Christians in Britain sought to revive their churches with the large-scale New Century Campaign. Organised by the Rev. Thomas Law, secretary of the National Council of Free Churches, the campaign was backed by 600 local Free Church Councils. Beginning with united missions in every district of London, the New Century Campaign branched into similar campaigns all over Britain. The crusade emphasised the gift of preaching, and was called one of the most remarkable ecclesiastical movements of its time.

Several of the era's most gifted British evangelists and pastors took part, including G. Campbell Morgan, whose sixty books including *The Practice of Prayer* are still widely read today. Only thirteen years old when he preached his first sermon, Morgan became the outstanding preacher and Bible expositor of the first half of the twentieth century.

Another well-known evangelist in the New Century Campaign was F. B. Meyer, whose sixty-year ministry included forty-one years as minister at two prominent London churches. Meyer also launched an evangelistic ministry which brought many down-and-out men from London's slums into the Kingdom of God.

Gipsy Rodney Smith was another gifted evangelist involved in the New Century Campaign. Born in a gipsy tent near Epping Forest in today's northeast section of Greater London, Smith – a self-taught preacher, writer and singer – joined The Salvation Army at the invitation of William Booth. Smith eventually travelled to many parts of the world to spread the Gospel, and is best known for mass evangelistic campaigns in Britain and America.

BILLY GRAHAM IN BRITAIN

The best-known evangelist in Britain during the second half of the twentieth century has been the American Billy

Graham. He led three major campaigns in England in the 1950s, 1960s and 1980s, with thousands coming to Christ.

Billy Graham's international recognition as an evangelist began during his 1949 Los Angeles crusade. Thirty-five years later, more than ninety million people had heard him personally, and hundreds of thousands had registered professions of faith in Christ.

Graham was one of the first evangelists to use motion pictures and television to communicate the Gospel around the world. Millions have heard him preach via radio and television broadcasts. Millions more have been reached through his films and books, his newspaper column, *Decision* magazine, and his weekly 'Hour of Decision' radio programme. An evangelist to the world, he has preached the Gospel in more than sixty countries, speaking before more people than any other man in history.

Graham's first major crusade in Britain was a twelve-week campaign in Harringay Arena from March through May in 1954. He preached six nights weekly for seventy-two nights, with his audiences filling the 12,000-seat sports palace each night. So many thousands were eager to hear him preach the Gospel that two and sometimes three evening services were necessary to handle the overflow. The campaign was sponsored by more than a thousand Greater London churches of all denominations, with two-thirds of them being Church of England.

The Harringay services were aired to capacity audiences in halls and churches in 400 communities throughout England, Scotland and Wales. Two million people heard Billy Graham preach the Gospel during the three-month campaign, with 40,000 making decisions for Christ.

Although mass evangelism was not always viewed as an effective method in Britain, the results at Harringay were astonishing. In 1955, a *British Weekly* survey revealed that 64 per cent of those who made decisions for Christ at Harringay were still regularly attending church a year after the crusade.

Graham returned to London for a crusade at Earls Court Arena in June 1966. The total attendance of 946,359 broke the record for the largest month-long crusade in history.

More than forty thousand people came forward, either to stand in front of the rostrum at Earls Court or in front of a huge cinema-size TV screen as enquirers.

THE 1980s – THE DECADE OF EVANGELISM

When British Christians with a vision for evangelism dubbed the 1980s the 'Decade of Evangelism', two major efforts for 1984 emerged: Luis Palau's Mission to London and Billy Graham's Mission England.

During his 1984 Mission England campaign, Graham preached in May, June and July for eight days each in Bristol, Sunderland, Birmingham and Liverpool; four days in Norwich and five days in Ipswich. He spoke to crowds totalling more than one million, and 96,982 people came forward.

After the campaign Graham said: 'This has been one of the highlights, maybe *the* highlight of my entire ministry.'[13]

Although many Britons opposed the idea of mass evangelism, and especially of two foreign evangelists coming to Britain during the same period, the *Birmingham Sunday Mercury* reported: 'If Billy Graham or Luis Palau . . . are prepared to give their time and their love and a large slice of their life to try to wake us out of our apathy . . . let us thank God for such men.'[14]

Billy Graham and Luis Palau stressed that they were having evangelistic campaigns in Britain simultaneously in cooperation to bring more Britons into the Kingdom of God.

Graham and Palau are good friends and long-time supporters of one another's ministry. As a teenager in Argentina, Palau received Graham's magazine reporting his successful London crusade of 1954. This magazine whetted Palau's appetite for mass evangelism, especially in using the media to reach the world with the Gospel.

When Palau went to the US as a young man, he was honoured to serve as the Spanish interpreter for Billy Graham's Central California Crusade in 1962.

At the Mission to London launching ceremony in Trafalgar Square in September 1983, Palau told a crowd of 8,000 Londoners that he and Billy Graham regularly pray together, especially for Mission England and Mission to London. Later the two evangelists sent British Christians a joint 1984 New Year's message: 'We ask you to pray for Mission England and Mission to London during 1984. We count on your prayer support for London and all of England during this important period of evangelism.'

In early 1984, three months before their respective British missions began, Graham wrote to Palau: 'I am thrilled at all that I heard concerning the preparations for the Mission to London. I also sense a moving of God's Spirit in various parts of England and believe that together we may see God do a new thing, at least for this generation, in England.'[15]

Chapter 3

WHY MASS EVANGELISM?
by Luis Palau

On many occasions Luis Palau has been asked if he believes mass evangelism is still effective in winning men and women to Jesus Christ. Palau responds in this chapter with a hearty 'Yes!'

Evangelists such as D. L. Moody, John Wesley, George Whitefield and Billy Graham have added hundreds of thousands to God's Kingdom through mass crusades. As long as the Lord raises up evangelists around the world with a passion for the masses, mass evangelism has a great future.

Although mass evangelism is widely criticised, it remains one of the most powerful evangelistic tools that God has given His people. This is especially true in today's mass media generation.

I believe the close of the twentieth century will be the church's most significant and exciting period for mass evangelism because mass evangelism utilises not only mass rallies, but also radio, television, films, video tapes, cassettes and all other modern communication media to reach the world for Jesus Christ.

Following are twenty-seven reasons why I emphatically believe in the future of mass evangelism.

REACHING THOUSANDS

1: City-wide crusade evangelism, practised in the power of the Holy Spirit, communicates the truth of God to multiplied thousands of people. The New Testament clearly states that this is God's deepest desire (Mark 13:10).

2: Through mass evangelism, cities and often nations become 'God-conscious'. An awareness of the Gospel sweeps across whole nations during mass evangelism, and a sense of expectancy touches the conscience of thousands. Conversations in restaurants, hotels and private homes often revolve around God, Jesus Christ and the Bible.

This 'God-consciousness' of a city-wide crusade becomes an amazing bridge to men's souls as Christians witness daily with authority. For many Christians, mass evangelism is the moment of spiritual renewal and dedication to Christ.

3: Mass evangelism grabs the attention of national leaders and gains a hearing for the Gospel in places otherwise less accessible. Leaders usually do not pay attention to the Gospel, but when they notice a mass movement of people or an impact in the media, they often listen.

4: Mass evangelism can reach the spiritually hungry people who are lost within our vast metropolitan areas. Like Cornelius in Acts 10, these people have been searching and waiting for the Good News to come to their attention. Thousands of these searchers are drawn to the massive movement of a crusade, respond to the Gospel, and are transformed by the power of Jesus Christ.

5: The world-wide population explosion demands crusade evangelism because a new generation is always coming of age. Even in a previously evangelised city, each new generation must be given the opportunity to respond to the Gospel.

'Preach the Gospel to every creature' was not a suggestion, but a command of our Lord. The Body of Christ cannot sit by quietly, functioning only to build itself up, without a specific effort to reach out to the sea of unbelievers.

6: Practised in the power of the Holy Spirit, mass evangelism gives Christians an opportunity to confront their neighbours with the marvellous saving grace of God. Many of the 150,000 people who die each day world-wide have never heard of salvation through Jesus Christ. Mass evangelism can change this desperation into hope by flooding a city with spiritual conversations and witnessing opportunities.

7: Mass evangelism has a future because neglected duty calls for extraordinary measures. The earth has never been saturated with the Gospel in the Church's 2,000-year history because not every Christian has evangelised and witnessed as the Lord commands us.

Even nations with religious freedom cannot say that every Christian is actively spreading the Good News. Mass evangelism is a necessary instrument used by God for stepping into the gap left by those Christians who do not share their faith.

8: Young people, otherwise indifferent to Christianity, are attracted by the mass crusade approach. Apparent peer approval draws them to the stadium and brings them under the message of Jesus Christ. Because more than 50 per cent of the world's population is under twenty-five years old, mass evangelism must be used to communicate Christ to the younger generation.

Since the days of D. L. Moody, young people have responded to mass evangelical movements. Even college students in most sophisticated universities will listen, debate and sometimes respond to the Gospel when they are confronted through a mass evangelistic effort.

9: Mass evangelism has a soil-testing function of revealing responsive and non-responsive populations. This aids local church planting and strategic decision-making by churches and missions.

10: Mass evangelism based on the Word of God helps the Body of Christ to present a strong, united front to a watching world. When directed by the Holy Spirit, city-wide crusades demolish barriers within the Body. Believers meeting for the first time or those who had nurtured animosities between each other begin to experience the love of God. Spiritual healing takes place in the Body of Christ when God works through mass evangelism.

The sense of God's presence and blessing among His people in a united effort can seldom be experienced under any other circumstance. Christians use mass evangelism to tell the world that we have a common core of biblical faith that binds us to Jesus Christ and to one another. The love that believers display in a city-wide crusade leaves a strong impression in the minds of the city's unbelievers.

11: Wisely executed, mass evangelism reaches 'the untouchables' with the Word of God. The 'untouchables' are the upper class and professionals who, in many nations, have not been evangelised. This also includes people in the arts and entertainment fields, along with the professors of the great universities.

Today's massive cities are difficult to evangelise. With the united action of believers, mass evangelism penetrates a city by all mass communication media available. Newspaper reports and radio and television broadcasts of the crusade cause even the most 'untouchable' citizens to be affected by the Word of God.

PROPHETIC VOICE OF GOD

12: Mass evangelism is the prophetic voice of God to a nation through His people. When carried out in the power of the Holy Spirit, it is a historic moment in which the authoritative, prophetic Word of God can shake a city numbering millions by forcing confrontation with the living, Almighty God.

This public preaching of Jesus Christ opens up a city, and that city can never again be quite the same because its people have heard the voice of the living God.

13: Mass evangelism practised in the power of the Holy Spirit dislodges the powers of darkness. Scripture teaches and experience demonstrates the existence of entrenched forces of darkness that dominate nations. When the Body of Christ proclaims the Gospel on a massive scale, the forces of darkness are disrupted, often dislodged, and have to flee before the power of Almighty God.

14: Mass evangelism unites Christians with great joy as they witness, pray, praise and worship God together. Although united campaigns are primarily aimed at the salvation of unbelievers, Christians have often been so thoroughly transformed that they refer to these campaigns as revivals.

15: Mass evangelism has a shepherding function towards the Christian community. Sometimes questions of Christian doctrine and practice go unanswered, but helpful Christian counselling begins when an evangelistic team, under the direction of God, launches a mass campaign. Practical biblical counselling is included in the training of crusade counsellors, ushers, choir members and children's workers.

16: Mass evangelistic efforts often revolutionise the self-images of individual Christians. The unity of thousands in a public stadium creates a sense of oneness with the Body of Christ in the hearts of lonely Christians.

17: The image of biblical Christianity is enhanced by mass evangelism. The masses have twisted views of Christianity, but the enormous impact of mass evangelism enhances the image of God's grace and goodness expressed in His Gospel.

18: Mass evangelism uses each gift of the Holy Spirit for the glory of God (Ephesians 4:11–12). A united evangelistic effort has room for every gift the Lord has bestowed on His Body.

19: City-wide crusades provide many Christians, including some ministers, that first-time opportunity of leading another person to Christ. During a crusade, a sense of spiritual power, the excitement, the harvest going on around them and the unusual movement of God in the city causes even timid Christians to discover that personal evangelism is the most exciting experience in the Christian life. For many believers who were indecisive about sharing their faith, the crusade marks the beginning of a lifetime witness.

20: Properly utilised, mass evangelism places the media at the service of a sovereign Creator. I believe that God allowed the invention of modern mass media for the purpose of sharing His truth, not for corrupting humanity. When films, telephones, radio, television and the press become God's instruments, they fulfil His holy purpose of redeeming and blessing humanity.

As the media report the crusade events, the Gospel breaks hardened and reactionary attitudes. Often unexpectedly, those who mould the thinking of the masses broadcast a

proper and clear vision of the truth of God through the
medium they control.

ENCOURAGING CHURCH GROWTH

21: Local churches grow numerically and spiritually. Mass
evangelism creates a sense of responsibility in existing
evangelical churches to plant new congregations. We have
seen scores of new congregations emerge through the work of
evangelistic campaigns in the last several years.

22: Many outstanding Christian leaders are the fruit of
mass evangelism. Calls to the ministry emerge again and
again during mass evangelistic campaigns. Dozens of men
converted to Christ during Billy Graham's 1954 London
Crusade and his 1955 Glasgow Crusade are in the ministry
today, and many played integral roles in Mission to London.

Teaching by example becomes a fruitful effect of the
crusade, and the younger generation is awakened with a
passion to reach out to the lost.

23: Mass evangelism opens doors for other forms of
evangelism and Bible teaching that may otherwise remain
closed. During mass crusades, believers and churches are
more willing to initiate various methods of Christian witness
and evangelism.

24: The public confession of faith reinforces the decision
to follow Christ in the mind and heart of the enquirer. Just as
the apostles called for public, visible baptism, so in mass
evangelism a public surrender to Christ speaks volumes.

25: Mass evangelism creates the climate for calls to justice
and honesty at all levels in a nation. This climate opens the
door for the Body of Christ to influence society as the salt of
the earth and the light of the world. Conversion of thousands
to Jesus Christ causes a transformation in the family and
business life of a nation. Mass evangelism supplies the vision
and creates the climate for these national changes.

26: Mass evangelism and revival walk arm in arm because
historically, God has used mass evangelism to kindle revivals.
John and Charles Wesley and George Whitefield led the great

evangelical revival of the eighteenth century across the British Isles and North America. God honoured their strenuous campaigning by converting thousands upon thousands to Christ.

Spiritual healing and renewal within the Body of Christ occur when God works through a united mass evangelistic campaign. The Lord showers blessings upon a land and its people when the 'brothers live together in unity! . . . For there the Lord bestows his blessing, even life for evermore' (Psalm 133:1,3).

27: Finally, a mass crusade conducted in the power of the Holy Spirit and proclaiming the truth of the Gospel glorifies God because:

1. It proclaims the glory of His name.
2. It exalts the person and the work of His Son.
3. It presents Christ's substitutionary death on the cross and His powerful resurrection from the dead.
4. It proclaims His power to transform individuals, families and nations.
5. It warns of judgment to come and of the living hope in the Father's house (John 14).

The Bible says, 'But thanks be to God, who always leads us in triumphal procession in Christ and through us spreads everywhere the fragrance of the knowledge of him. For we are to God the aroma of Christ among those who are being saved and those who are perishing' (2 Corinthians 2:14–15).

God is glorified and pleased when we spread the fragrance of the knowledge of Him everywhere.

Does mass evangelism have a future? My answer is a resounding 'Yes!' I believe that mass evangelism, practised in the power of the Holy Spirit and proclaiming the true Gospel of Jesus Christ, will move both those who practise it and those who observe it to exclaim in the words of St Paul: 'To the King eternal, immortal, invisible, the only God, be honour and glory for ever and ever. Amen' (1 Timothy 1:17).

Chapter 4

BRITAIN – A CHRISTIAN NATION?

'All around us are signs of moral decay and apathy,' Luis Palau told the crowd at QPR stadium. 'Moral standards are being blown to the winds. But I don't believe this is what people really want.'

Palau explained that because many British people have turned their backs on God and moved away from Christian values, the nation is experiencing fatal consequences – a rising violent crime rate, an increase in sexual immorality, a glut of pornography, and escalating drug and alcohol abuse. Quieter results – but just as fatal – are divorce, single-parent families, and loneliness.

In the autumn of 1983 the Luis Palau Evangelistic Team asked 1,372 women in six areas of London to list the main problems they encountered in their daily lives. In each area, violence was listed as the number one problem. The startling results hint of the violent conditions on London's streets, and the fear felt by the people who live there.

The number two problem listed by these women was loneliness. C. S. Lewis wrote in his book *The Four Loves*, 'As soon as we are fully conscious we discover loneliness.'[1]

A Market and Opinion Research International poll for London's *Sunday Times Magazine* estimated that 25 per cent of the entire British population is lonely – with women, the elderly, the young, the single parent, the widowed and the unemployed most at risk.

Other problems that ranked high included fear, depression, lack of love, living in a society indifferent to God, and difficulties in raising children. The women's responses present a bleak picture of the fast-paced, yet isolated lifestyle in London.

In 1981 a total of 157,000 divorces were granted in the
United Kingdom, almost double the number of divorces in
1971. Second marriages are also collapsing in increasing
proportions. By 1981 more than one in five of all second
marriages ended in divorce.

In June 1983 the *Daily Telegraph* reported that one in eight
of all British children are raised by single parents. The Study
Commission on the Family reported that Britain has about
one million single-parent families, almost double the number
twelve years ago. The report indicated that one British child
in five has parents who will divorce before the child is
sixteen.[2]

A recent survey found that British youth have an increasingly liberal view toward such issues as premarital sex,
homosexuality and abortion.

Unmarried British men and women living together – now
an acceptable lifestyle in Britain and much of the West –
increased by 300 per cent from 1970 to 1980. In first marriages performed in 1979–80, more than one in six women
had lived with their husbands before the wedding.

From 1971 to 1981, legal abortions in England and Wales
increased by 36 per cent. Girls under twenty years old
accounted for more than one in four of the 129,000 legal
abortions in 1981.

DISAPPEARING MORAL STANDARDS

Many Christian leaders are asking: 'What has happened to
Britain's moral standards?'

'Children must be taught a set of moral standards,' said
Palau. 'They must have a code to live up to. How else will
they become responsible adults? Discipline and morality
must begin and be instilled in the home. If children have a
secure home life they can face all sorts of outside nasties.'

'Outside nasties' abound in Britain, and especially London. The number of ultra-violent and pornographic videos in
Britain has risen sharply since 1982. The report *Video Violence and Children*, recently published by the Parliamentary

Group Video Enquiry, claims that hundreds of thousands of British children have viewed legally obscene films and that more than 40 per cent of children over five in England and Wales have seen one or more video nasties like *Driller Killer*, depicting scenes of sadistic and horrific violence.

Dr Clifford Hill, research director of the Enquiry, warned: 'We may have already done so much harm in poisoning the minds of children that we may be producing the most violent generation of young people and young adults in modern history.'[3]

The statistics strengthen Dr Hill's statement. A recent news report stated that of all age groups in England and Wales, fourteen- to sixteen-year-olds commit the most crimes per thousand population. Boys under twenty-one commit 40 per cent of the sexual offences and 58 per cent of the total robberies committed by males. Crime rates for girls are also increasing, with girls under twenty-one committing the majority of the 74,000 thefts by females.

Drug and alcohol abuse is escalating in Britain. The *Sunday Times* reported on 2 October 1983 that Britain's volume of contraband heroin increased by 700 per cent from 1977 to 1981. As illegal drugs become available to more people, the number of drug addicts in Britain is also increasing. Although 4,700 drug addicts were reported to the Home Office in 1982, the police, customs officials and voluntary organisations concerned with drug abuse agreed that the real number of drug addicts in Britain was between 40,000 and 50,000, with 70 per cent of these addicted to heroin.[4]

The use of household solvents or glue to obtain a 'high' is also escalating, especially among younger children. In July 1983 the Department of Health and Social Security reported that 104 people had died from glue abuse in the previous two years. *Evangelism Today* reported in March 1984 that 'every six days a child dies in Britain as a direct result of the craze for sniffing solvent'. Police and social workers believe the true figure is higher.[5]

Drugs. Crime. Violence. Pornography. Abortion. Divorce. Is Britain a Christian nation today?

The Rev. Clive Calver, general secretary of The Evangelical

Alliance, summed up Britain's problem in a nutshell: 'We are not a Christian nation. We haven't been a Christian nation for a long time. We've simply maintained the fabric of Christianity.'

Palau said: 'I feel that if London is not turned around very soon, England could collapse socially, politically, and economically. Although I don't want to sound overly dramatic, it's been sobering to see that England and all of Britain seem to be at a spiritual crossroads. Today England, continental Europe and many more of the world's free countries are moving swiftly towards secularism. The breakdown of the family and the plummeting moral and ethical standards demand that the Christian Church speak out.'

But it has been difficult for the struggling church in Britain to be heard. As Calver stated, 'Christianity, or Church worship at least, has been declining in this nation for sixty years.'

EMPTY CHURCHES

Attitudes to the Bible, God, and the Church, a survey published by Britain's Bible Society in June 1983, supports the statement that Britain is no longer a Christian nation. The survey was conducted to provide evidence of the country's depressed religious climate prior to Mission to London and Billy Graham's Mission England.

The survey includes churches in England between 1975 and 1979, and was compiled by Peter Brierley, European director of Missions Advanced Research and Communications Centre, a research branch of the organisation World Vision.

The survey reports that one in three of England's 39,000 Trinitarian churches has a Sunday morning congregation of less than twenty-six people, with an average Sunday congregation of seventy-six. Almost one-fifth of London's 2,870 Protestant churches have twenty-five or fewer members. Forty-seven per cent have less than fifty members, and 76 per cent less than a hundred.

The only Trinitarian churches which have actually *increased* over recent years include the West Indian and African, Pentecostal/Holiness, Independent and Orthodox churches.

In comparison, most non-Trinitarian religions have grown tremendously. Spiritualists rose from 45,000 to 52,000 from 1970 to 1980. The numbers of Jehovah's Witnesses and Mormons in the United Kingdom increased by at least 20,000 members each in the same decade. The most dramatic increases of the decade occurred among the Sikhs, who doubled from 75,000 to 150,000, and the Muslims, who multiplied from 250,000 to a booming 600,000 in 1980.

The enormous increases in non-Trinitarian church membership stem mainly from the influx of immigrants from Africa, the Caribbean, India, Bangladesh, the Far East, the Mediterranean, and Pakistan, whose numbers rose by more than 35 per cent in the last decade.

Many previous evangelistic strategies of the Christian church have focused on reaching people associated with the church. But today many Londoners are not on the fringe of the church. In August 1983, *Today* magazine reported that more than one million Londoners are from other religious and cultural backgrounds, mostly from the Indian subcontinent. In some London boroughs, people have never heard the name Jesus Christ. London is a fantastic mission field for the Christian faith.

Although many Britons claim to be connected with a church, actual church attendance is very low. Only 10 per cent of Londoners questioned said they attend church once a week or more, and the national average is only 15 per cent. Some researchers believe consistent church attendance could be as low as 4 per cent. Fifty-six per cent of the English attend church only at christenings, weddings or funerals. Almost 70 per cent of England's male population attend church once a year or less.

Tom Houston, former executive director of the Bible Society said: 'Almost two in five people questioned feel the church needs to change its image if it is to attract people.'[6]

Calver agreed: 'Some people say the answer to the decline

in church attendance in England is to enliven the church and make it more exciting and interesting, especially for the young people.'

Calver, in his mid-thirties, added: 'Ninety per cent of my generation and younger have never rejected Christ. They've never heard the Gospel. That makes England an incredible mission field.'

Reaching England's youth is a difficult task for the church. The sixteen to twenty-four age group has the lowest church attendance in England, with only 10 per cent attending at least once a week and 27 per cent attending never or practically never.

Houston stated: 'If the church wants to communicate with the people today, it must climb down off the pedestal of its own unflinching orthodoxy and take steps to whet the appetites of people for the Bible. Reading the Bible is one of the keys of improving the Christian climate. Once the church gets people reading the Bible, they will develop a better attitude towards God and the church as well as the Bible itself.'[7]

Very few of the English actually read the Bible regularly. Although about 12 per cent of the population say they read the Bible at least once a week, 70 per cent say they never or hardly ever do. Of those who regularly attend church, 32 per cent seldom or never read the Bible themselves.

THE AUTHORITY OF THE BIBLE

During Mission to London the authority of the Bible became a popular issue throughout the city. People from various cultural, social and religious backgrounds debated whether the Bible was God's authoritative and inspired Word. The Bible's authority is questioned not only by the general public, but also by many clergy.

Palau told an audience of British Christians: 'When I hear people who profess to be Christians questioning whether the Bible is God's Word, I can't help but wonder if Christians today worship too small a God. If God is God, then couldn't

He write a book that is without error?' he asked. 'Of course He could – and He did. The Bible is authoritative because it is *God's* Word, not man's.'

Palau told his audience at QPR stadium: 'London's churches are empty because people deny the authority of the Bible. They denigrate Jesus Christ. The Bible is not just another religious book. It is the Word of God, inspired by the Holy Spirit. It is the authority for everything we do and say as Christians.

'Christians need to recover the authority of Scripture or the churches will continue to be empty. People are looking for leadership from the Church. If we have no authority, all we have is "I think, I think, I think".'

THE BISHOP JENKINS CONTROVERSY

A heated controversy emerged in the midst of Mission to London when the Right Rev. David Jenkins, bishop-elect for Durham, voiced his doubts in the media on the reliability of some foundational biblical doctrines.

On London Weekend Television's *Credo* programme, Jenkins said: 'The Virgin Birth, I'm pretty clear, is a story told after the event in order to express and symbolise a faith that this Jesus was a unique event from God . . . I wouldn't put it past God to arrange a virgin birth if he wanted, but I very much doubt if he would, because it seems to be contrary to the way in which he deals with persons and brings his wonders out of natural personal relationships.'[8]

Jenkins said that although he believed in the resurrection, he didn't believe that Jesus physically rose from the tomb. He also said that he believed Jesus was divine, but added that other Christians didn't have to believe the same.

Jenkins said: 'I think it quite likely that Jesus performed miracles or was thought to perform miracles,' but added that even Jesus looked at miracles cautiously.[9]

After the programme, conservatives questioned Jenkins's remarks, but the bishop-elect stated that it was because of his faith that he raised the controversial questions.

Two months later – at the height of QPR – another *Credo* programme broadcast survey results stating that a third of the Church of England's bishops agreed with Jenkins's statements.

Jenkins's appointment as the country's fourth most senior Anglican cleric thrust the church into a heated controversy. British Christians rallied in an unsuccessful attempt to stop the consecration of Jenkins which took place on 6 July at York Minster.

The *Economist* noted 'how very different' were the doubts of the Anglican bishops from 'the simple faith that has been offered this month to a largely heathen Britain by two foreign evangelists.'

Citing the successful Palau and Graham campaigns, the magazine continued: 'Both evangelists deal in certainties. They know that Jesus is the rock of salvation, and that the Bible, all of it, is the word of God . . .

'Perhaps the bishops of the Church of England should go to football stadiums more often.'[10]

In the face of such evidence of Christianity's poor health in Britain, Palau affirmed: 'Like Paul, we need to think strategically if the whole world is to hear the voice of God. I believe the nation that could perhaps best fan such a movement of God world-wide is Britain. But first,' he added, 'her people need to once again hear and believe God's voice themselves.'[11]

Chapter 5

BURDEN FOR BRITAIN

Luis Palau stepped to the microphone and said: 'I am delighted to be here in London. I have a special regard for Britain. You know, my grandfather was Scottish. But most of all, it was through British missionaries that I came to know Christ . . .'

With this introduction, Palau began telling the exciting story of his boyhood in Argentina and his years of ministry in Latin America which grew into an extensive ministry with team members and regional offices world-wide. Foremost in this story are Palau's dreams of leading millions to faith in Jesus Christ.

Palau was born in Argentina in 1934, the first child of parents who were loving, but not Christians. His father refused to attend church. His mother, the organist of the local parish church, longed to know God personally.

Neither of his parents heard the Gospel until they met Charles Rogers. Rogers was a self-supporting missionary who went to Argentina to win people to Christ. Palau's mother accepted Christ through the witness of Mr Rogers, but his father continued to reject the Gospel. Yet his curiosity led him to hide in the shadows outside the small chapel Sunday after Sunday, listening to the missionary's sermons, and quietly sneaking away before the end of the service so no one would see him there.

As Palau tells it: 'One Sunday Dad finally entered the chapel, sat with my mother, and during the middle of the service, stood to proclaim: "I receive Jesus Christ as my only and sufficient Saviour." Then he sat down.

'Mr Rogers was so startled that he stopped preaching for a

few minutes. My mother nearly fainted. First she was embarrassed, but then she was so glad that he had finally accepted Christ.'

Both of Palau's parents became active evangelicals. Palau grew up attending Sunday school and church, but he still didn't know Jesus Christ personally.

When he was eight years old, his father sent him to a private British boarding school in Argentina. During a summer holiday when he was twelve, Palau reluctantly attended a camp organised by one of his British teachers to win boys to Christ. Frank Chandler, a British counsellor, led Palau to the Lord one rainy night as they sat on a log high in the mountains of Argentina. Palau was only a child, but he knew he had eternal life.

Two years earlier, his father had died of a sudden illness. The family plunged from prosperity to deep poverty, but Palau was able to graduate from St Alban's College in Buenos Aires in 1954. Then he supported his mother and younger sisters by working in a bank. Palau was encouraged by his mother to study the Bible extensively and become involved in an evangelism ministry through tent meetings and radio broadcasts. With a passion to reach out to the lost, he desired to spread the Gospel to all of Argentina.

Palau said: 'I was in Argentina in 1954 when somebody sent me the bulletins from Billy Graham's London crusade at Harringay Arena. Even then I knew that some day we would have a crusade in London. That was thirty years ago.'

In 1961 two American pastors helped to bring Palau to the United States to enrol in the graduate course at Multnomah School of the Bible in Portland, Oregon. There he planned to receive solid Bible training before returning to Argentina for a lifetime ministry.

At Multnomah, Palau met Patricia Scofield, whom he married after his graduation in 1961. Their union would produce four sons: twins Kevin and Keith born in 1963; Andrew in 1966; and Stephen in 1969.

The same year they were married, the Palaus joined the California-based missions organisation Overseas Crusades. By 1964 they were working hard evangelising in villages and towns in Colombia. In 1966 Palau had his first major crusade in Bogotá, Colombia's capital. The response was enthusiastic. Now he dreamed of reaching all of Latin America for Christ.

The following year he began building a solid evangelistic team of his own, a group of godly men and women dedicated to spreading the Gospel to the masses.

INCREASING THE VISION

Palau explained: 'At first God gave me vision to preach to the masses in Argentina, and later to all of Latin America. I thought my vision was big enough, but through the years God expanded my dream to reach millions world-wide. This desire to win people around the world to Jesus Christ is the foundation of the Luis Palau Evangelistic Team.'

In 1978 the Luis Palau Evangelistic Team left Overseas Crusades to form a separate organisation dedicated to world-wide evangelism.

In dependence upon God, the Palau Team has a threefold vision:

1) Winning as many people as possible to Jesus Christ throughout the world.
2) Emphasising with the church the principles of victorious Christian living to stimulate, revive and mobilise the church to continuous, effective evangelism, follow-up and church growth.
3) Influencing Christianity world-wide, holding high the banner of biblical evangelism, so that the church's commitment to evangelism will never die.

In countries where Palau crusades are organised, the team emphasises involving each local Christian, establishing new congregations, and stimulating growth in existing churches.

In saturating a city or nation with the Gospel of Christ, the team uses every form of mass media available: television, radio, the press, Bible literature, tracts and films, plus all forms of person-to-person evangelism.

The team's communications department has made great strides in furthering the Gospel. When the Lord opened the door for radio evangelism in Latin America in 1965, Palau began his continent-wide daily radio programmes *Cruzada* and *Luis Palau Responde*. Today these programmes are broadcast on 160 radio stations in Latin America, and reach an estimated audience of fifteen million people in more than twenty countries.

The English radio programme *Luis Palau Responds* is broadcast in the United States, New Zealand, the British West Indies, Swaziland, the Philippines, Ecuador and the Netherlands Antilles. The team has also produced several evangelistic films – forty in Spanish and five in English.

The Luis Palau Team also uses the written word to spread God's Word around the world. In 1972 the team published the first issue of *Cruzada*, a quarterly news magazine for Spanish-speaking people. *Continente Nuevo*, a Spanish magazine for Latin American pastors, was first published in 1978. The first issue of *Briefing*, the team's news magazine for English-speaking readers, was published in 1979.

Palau has also written five Spanish books and sixteen booklets. He regularly contributes an answer column to twenty Latin American newspapers and magazines. He has written ten books in English, some of which have been translated into Dutch, Swedish, German, Portuguese, Finnish and Afrikaans.

In addition to world-wide crusades and the media and publications departments, the team's growing ministry also includes family counselling centres, counselling by post and telephone, missionary and pastors' conferences, church growth training, Bible teaching and schools of evangelism and communication.

The team's nineteen years of ministry include more than one hundred campaigns in thirty-eight nations. Palau has preached the Gospel to a cumulative audience of six million people in person, and countless millions more via radio and television. More than 224,000 people have registered public decisions for Christ through the team's ministry. The largest single audience in the team's history - 700,000 people – gathered in Guatemala City on 28 November 1982 to hear him preach the Gospel. On 18 November 1984 the largest number of decisions for Christ made in a single meeting – just over three thousand – were recorded in Lima, Peru.

Although Luis Palau and his team continue to spread the Gospel to many parts of the world, Palau feels a special burden for Britain. One of his reasons for this is that British missionaries led him and his family to Christ.

He said: 'For me, coming to Britain is like paying a debt that I've owed for many years. I feel burdened to do for the British what they did for me – point the way to Jesus Christ.'

Palau explained that when Moody was leading the first Mission to London in 1875, Christian businessmen presented him with this challenge: 'Shake London and the world is shaken.' The same is true today.

He said: 'Reaching London for Christ can set off a chain reaction for the Gospel in all of Britain, Europe and the world.'

TESTING THE WATER IN BRITAIN

Palau's way to Britain was opened in 1975 when he participated in Eurofest '75, a youth congress in Brussels, sponsored by the Billy Graham Evangelistic Association. Through contacts made at the congress, he toured twelve European nations with a group of British musicians, and the following year he toured sixteen British cities. It was during these trips to Britain in 1976 that he discovered the country's lethargic spiritual condition. He summed up Britain's problem in one sentence: 'I see plenty of religion, but not much Christianity.'

Palau began to pray that the Lord would allow him to preach the Gospel in Britain. The Lord quickly answered these prayers with five major campaigns and several smaller evangelistic outreaches in Britain in the next six years.

Major campaigns prior to Mission to London were in Cardiff, Aberdeen, Ayrshire, Lanarkshire, Glasgow and Leeds. Attendance totalled 431,000, with 11,900 making public Christian commitments.

After the Glasgow crusade, the chairman the Rev. William Alston said: 'A few years ago, I felt as if God had abandoned Britain and we deserved it. But this crusade has shown that God is not dead and that there can be no argument against a changed life in Christ. This was indeed a people's crusade which brought joy and much-needed unity to the churches here. We've been given a taste of what God can do and now we must continue to work together to maintain this momentum.'[1]

The magnitude of the success at Leeds was discovered by a 1983 study which reported that several months after the Leeds campaign, 82 per cent of those who had made Christian commitments had continued following the Lord. The most astonishing statistic was that 100 per cent of the university students who had responded to the invitation at Leeds were still regularly attending church.[2]

In addition to speaking at these major British crusades, Palau also ministered at several smaller-scale evangelistic meetings in Britain.

During a 1981 British tour called Our God Reigns, he spoke at fifteen youth rallies in two weeks, with 2,700 young people registering Christian commitments. More than fifteen thousand young people gathered in London's Royal Albert Hall during this tour to hear the evangelist speak at three major rallies.

In 1979, 1980 and 1983 Palau was the keynote speaker at Britain's Spring Harvest, an annual national youth congress on evangelism. Britain's youth and Christian leaders responded enthusiastically to his straightforward messages.

Eric Delve, associate evangelist for phase one of Mission to London, said: 'Luis has been a terrific influence on me and on the other young leaders in this country because what he has constantly said to us is, "Go for it. We *can* see Britain really touched for Christ in this generation."'

A month after the Glasgow crusade, Derek Williams, then editor of *Today* magazine, wrote: 'The Luis Palau Glasgow crusade is over. It did not fulfil all the wildest dreams of its organisers. But, apart from the inestimable benefit to the 5,000 or so people who responded to the evangelist's call to Christian commitment, there was one overwhelming result. It put large-scale evangelism back on the British map, and proved that it still has a part to play in the church's outreach to a tired and troubled land.'[3]

The Rev. Clive Calver, Evangelical Alliance general secretary, said: 'I just think Luis lays it on the line, that he's honest and straight. That's why he appeals to the British, because he doesn't duck the issues. He actually speaks to where we are in our day and generation, and the common people hear him gladly for that reason.'

An even greater opportunity for Palau to minister in Britain came in 1981, when a delegation of London evangelical leaders travelled to the team's Glasgow crusade to extend an invitation for a massive London crusade. The team accepted, and immediately began preparing for the most complex campaign in its history, with a vision to 'let all of London hear the voice of God'.

Palau said: 'In 1979 when we first began planning a London crusade, I was campaigning in Australia as an associate of Billy Graham. In a hotel in Sydney I told Billy my hopes for a London crusade. We both got on our knees and we prayed together. Billy poured out his heart for London and all of Britain. Then he prayed that the Lord would use me in London.'

SECTION TWO

GEARING UP FOR
MISSION TO LONDON

Chapter 6

CULTIVATING THE VISION

'Stop a moment and consider the impact a revival in London would have on the rest of the world,' Luis Palau wrote in a letter to British Christians.

'I believe if London were evangelised, the whole world would soon know it. But how are we to do it? How can we begin to affect London with all its millions? Certainly an evangelist and his team cannot do it alone. It takes the whole Body of Christ working together, inspired by the Holy Spirit, to impact a whole city with the Gospel. We must organise, plan and prepare.'

In the spring of 1980 the organisation, planning and preparation for a major evangelistic mission in London had begun under the title New Way London. Sponsored by Britain's Evangelical Alliance as part of its Nationwide Initiative on Evangelism, and established at the request of London's churches, New Way London was a group of London Christians praying for God's guidance regarding a major evangelistic thrust in their city. The group's strategy called for waves of evangelism in the 1980s – dubbed the Decade of Evangelism. The group quickly began serious strategic planning for a large-scale campaign.

The leaders of New Way London realised the importance of obtaining local church support for the mission. In the autumn of 1980 300 ministers who gathered in City Temple were presented with the vision of asking a recognised evangelist to lead a massive campaign in London. An overwhelming 98 per cent of these ministers shared a positive initial reaction to the proposal.

EARLY PLANNING STAGES

The Evangelical Alliance appointed a New Way London
steering committee to invite Palau to London. Dr Clifford
Hill, then national director of evangelism for the Evangelical
Alliance, became the first director of New Way London. Hill
and his wife Monica, then national secretary for church
growth, were instrumental in inviting Luis Palau to London
for a major campaign.

Hill said: 'I thought that if one man could reach London it
was Luis. Luis has a very contemporary message and the
kind of personality that appeals to Londoners.'

A key member of the steering committee was Michael
Penny, a native Londoner whose background included seven
years with the Church Pastoral Aid Society. Penny first met
Palau when he attended Palau's 1981 Glasgow crusade, and
when the evangelist came over to meet the steering committee in 1981 he asked Penny to join his team and to direct
the London campaign. The team and New Way London
were joined to organise the massive London crusade.

To ensure that the greatest possible number of church
leaders be involved in the mission, Palau requested a wider
invitation from London's ministers. This was obtained by
the spring of 1981, and by October Penny was organising the
campaign, now known as Mission to London.

A headquarters office was set up in one small room at 112
City Road with no money, no staff, and not even a desk. By
faith, Penny hired a secretary during his first week and
together they prayed for her salary. As the staff gradually
increased, they met each morning for prayer.

The Lord continually answered their prayers. Financial
support grew as London's Christian businessmen caught the
mission's vision for reaching all of London for Christ. Staff,
offices and equipment were added gradually. Almost everything in the office was donated by Christians eager to help in
spreading the Gospel to London. Later a computer was
purchased to handle growing organisational needs. And the
computer salesman was the first Mission to London convert.

The next step was prayerfully to select a Mission to

London executive committee to oversee the campaign. By January 1982 this had been done, and in February they began discussing the basic structure and dates of the mission. The executive committee eventually decided on a two-part campaign: phase one missions throughout Greater London in September and October 1983, and phase two city-wide rallies in a large, centrally located stadium in the summer of 1984.

At the official announcement of Mission to London in the Royal Albert Hall in March 1982, Palau explained the mission's vision and strategy to 4,000 Christians representing almost 500 London churches. Congratulating the mission's organisers on the size of their vision, he shared his excitement for their plans – and particularly for local church preparation in phase one: 'I believe the area missions in 1983 will enable that preparation to be carried out thoroughly. This should mean an even greater impact for the major meetings in 1984 – bringing more blessing.'

NINE AREA MISSIONS

By May 1982 mission organisers envisioned up to nine area missions in the first phase in 1983, but they didn't know how to choose the mission sites. Michael Penny, who had become the official director of Mission to London, explained that dividing London into squares and randomly choosing mission sites 'would have been an absolute disaster because people would have accused us of imposing the mission. It had to come from the grass roots, from people in the areas. Londoners would feel it wasn't their mission if it were imposed upon them.'

In a meeting at the Mission to London headquarters, mission organisers shared with church leaders the vision of taking the Gospel to London through smaller area missions. Each potential mission area was asked to meet three conditions: acquire significant local church support, cooperate with the central Mission to London committee, and accept responsibility for the local expenditures.

By July nine area missions plus two larger meetings were planned for phase one in the autumn of 1983.

By September 1982 separate committees were formed for each aspect of the mission – including ministries of prayer, counselling, follow-up and youth work. To further disperse the work load, an identical structure was formed for each of the nine areas sponsoring local missions. These local groups worked under the leadership of the central committees. By February 1983 700 committee members in nineteen committees were actively developing the mammoth vision.

Palau spurred readers of the *Christian Herald* to catch the vision for evangelism: 'The Lord doesn't intend for us to sit idle and simply dream of what could happen for His glory. He wants us to plan great plans so that dreams will come true.'

'What about you?' he asked. 'Are you expecting great things from God? Or are you sitting around? If it's true that the Lord Jesus wants the Gospel preached world-wide, then we can't remain passive.'

WORKING WITH CHURCHES

Due to the great size of Mission to London, Palau eagerly sought the prayerful counsel of godly men such as the Archbishop of Canterbury, Dr Robert Runcie; the Bishop of London, Dr Graham Leonard; and Bishop John Taylor of Saint Albans.

On several occasions Palau met with London ministers to share his vision of reaching London's millions with the Gospel. In November 1981 he met with 500 ministers at All Souls Church, Langham Place, to share the biblical basis for crusade evangelism and to discuss the crusade's strategy. During this trip he also shared the mission's vision with the Bishop of London, the Archbishop of Canterbury and the Speaker of the House of Commons.

When the Bishop of London heard the vision of Mission to London he said: 'I think I could really get behind the mission because you are going to get everyone working on it.'

CULTIVATING THE VISION   61

Palau stated: 'The mission is not just the work of my team, but also of the churches of London. Especially the churches.'

Working closely with local churches has always been absolutely imperative during the Palau team's crusades. The situation was no different in London, where Palau stressed the importance of unity between mission organisers and London churches.

Ministers' seminars, church growth courses for ministers and lay leaders, Christian life and service classes, and rallies for church representatives illustrate how closely Mission to London was tied into local churches to achieve the most fruitful mission possible.

When Mission to London was first proposed in 1980, less than five hundred churches shared this vision of reaching their city for Christ. But by the autumn of 1983 more than one thousand London churches backed phase one of the mission, and only seven months later, a month before the central meetings began, more than seventeen hundred Greater London churches had joined the mission forces. The unity stimulated among these churches during the mission will bear fruit for years to come.

Peter Meadows, executive director of Mission to London, wrote to Palau in early 1983: 'The ministers' conferences have been thrilling, with a great air of expectancy and men leaving with fresh vision and commitment.'

A *Baptist Times* article reported that Mission to London had stimulated evangelistic witness and training for several former Spurgeon's College students who had entered the ministry.

With church support and an organisational framework in place, the next task for Mission to London was to locate actual structures for each of the nine area missions. Large tents, some with seating capacities exceeding three thousand, were assembled on heaths and parks for most of the area missions, while three of the missions were held in arenas and theatres. Wembley Arena was the site for the two larger meetings which climaxed the first phase of Mission to London in October 1983.

IN SEARCH OF A STADIUM

But mission organisers encountered difficulty in finding a large, ideally located covered stadium for the central meetings in 1984.

Penny's search for a stadium ended when a former press aide to the Queen suggested Queen's Park Rangers' football stadium in heavily populated West London. Penny was told the stadium would accommodate more than twenty thousand people during non-athletic events by seating hundreds on the artificial turf on the pitch.

When Palau first saw the football stadium in 1982 he was impressed with its clean attractiveness and convenient location to public transport. The stadium also had a roof over the seats to protect visitors from the rain.

Penny met with the stadium's financial director, and was asked if Mission to London had money to book the stadium. 'No,' replied Penny, gulping. 'We have no money.'

'Well, how are you going to pay for it?'

'Well, the true answer is that we are going to pray for the money. God has supplied needs for this sort of ministry in other countries, and I believe God will supply our needs here.'

Penny looked him straight in the eye and said: 'How do you feel about that one for a proposition?'

The financial director scratched his head. 'I believe you. You're on.'

The gears were in motion. The stadium was secured. Committees were planning. Churches were praying. The vision of Mission to London spread quickly as Christians around the city were mobilised for the enormous evangelistic campaign.

In January 1983 10,000 people packed London's Royal Albert Hall for Prepare the Way, two launching meetings for Luis Palau's Mission to London and Billy Graham's Mission England. During the ceremony, which was organised by British Youth for Christ, Palau spoke on film to motivate London Christians to prayer and action: 'Let all of London hear the voice of God. This should be the motto of this mission. This should be the burning desire in all our hearts, that every man, woman, young person and child in London hears the voice of God clearly during Mission to London.'

He added: 'The Lord wants to bless Britain in a marvellous and superlative way. And He's going to do it, I believe, as each member of the Body of Christ wakes up to his responsibilities to minister within his church and evangelise those who still need to hear the voice of God. Won't you join me in praying and working towards that end?

'This is the hour for London,' he urged. 'Now is the time to evangelise.'

The public launch of Mission to London was a Trafalgar Square rally where 8,000 Londoners prayed for their city.

Below left: Luis Palau speaking with Sikhs in Southall.

Below right: A larger-than-life photograph for the Wembley Arena billboard.

Phase One concluded with two packed meetings at the Wembley Arena.

The 'Bring Your Doubts' advertising theme became a talking point and helped Christians to invite their friends.

An interview with Thames News at QPR. Luis Palau was interviewed by dozens of British journalists for television, radio, newspapers and magazines.

More than 18,000 children, parents, and counsellors heard Luis Palau at the Rainbow Special at QPR.

Let the whole of London hear the voice of God! During the Mission Luis Palau preached the Gospel all around Greater London.

Cliff Richard sang at three QPR meetings.

Musician Dave Pope, founder of the Saltmine Trust.

Above left: At a mission children's rally, an example of the mission's outreach to specialized groups which effectively reached large segments of Londoners for Christ.

Above right: On several evenings the crowds flowed on to the pitch as thousands came to hear Luis Palau at QPR.

Below: Explaining the Gospel.

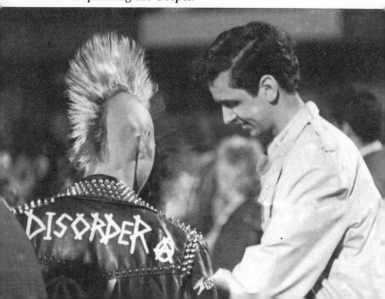

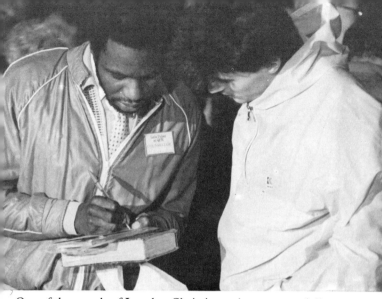

One of thousands of London Christians who were specially trained to serve as Mission to London counsellors.

Billy Graham with Luis and Pat Palau and their two younger sons Stephen and Andrew.

The London Community Gospel Choir made frequent visits to QPR.

The final night at QPR. The massive crowds demonstrate the variety of the thousands of every age, race, ethnic, and religious background who heard the Gospel during Mission to London.

Chapter 7

MOBILISING MULTITUDES

Mission to London mobilised a massive army of 15,000 Christians to reach their city for Christ. One mission administrator said: 'Luis crystallised what can be done in evangelisation, especially in mobilising people.'

People were needed to pray, motivate local churches, raise finances, type letters and write the mission's *Countdown* magazine. The mission also needed sound technicians, electricians, musicians, cameramen and journalists as well as stewards, counsellors and choir members.

Still others were needed to clean the stadium grounds, erect and dismantle huge tents, man the QPR turnstiles, distribute invitations, fill coaches with people to bring to the stadium, and recruit yet more volunteers. Thousands of Christians donated their time, talent and treasures to make Mission to London a reality.

A few months prior to QPR, Peter Meadows, who succeeded Michael Penny as Mission to London's executive director in 1983, announced the mission's need for 6,000 choir members, 2,000 stewards, 15,000 bridge-builders, 600 advisers, 7,500 counsellors, 1,600 church representatives, 2,000 task force members, 300 coaches to QPR each night, and volunteers to visit four million homes to extend personal invitations to the mission. The numbers seemed incredible.

Although some workers travelled from as far away as Finland, North America, Australia and Ghana to participate in the mission, the majority came from churches in London and the Home Counties. Vocations represented included mechanics, executives, housewives, ministers, students, missionaries, teachers, policemen and the unemployed.

No one was too young or too old to help with the mission. Ten-year-old children and ninety-year-old great-grandmothers donated their time and money to the mission. Race was not a factor either, as black, white, yellow and brown all worked together in one body during Mission to London. Nor was denomination a factor. Anglicans, Baptists, Methodists, Pentecostals and many others united to proclaim the Gospel to their city.

THE LUIS PALAU EVANGELISTIC TEAM

John McWilliam, director of international crusades and a seventeen-year Palau team veteran, supervised the London crusade for eighteen months, often working for months on end in London.

The Rev. Jim Williams, the team's vice president and director of counselling, taught family counsellor training classes in London. Williams also directed the family counselling centre which provided free in-depth biblical counselling at the crusade site.

Kari Lindqvist from Finland had so superbly organised Palau's 1982 crusade in Helsinki that he was invited to join the Palau team to help in coordinating Mission to London in early 1983.

Americans Bill and Joan MacLeod lived in London for twenty months to prepare for the crusade. Before Mission to London, MacLeod coordinated Palau crusades in Aberdeen and Ayrshire. In London he addressed churches, youth groups and Christian Unions to enthuse them about evangelising their city.

Albert and Roberta Wollen pastored Luis Palau's home church in Portland, Oregon, for more than thirty years before retiring in 1982 and moving to London to help with the mission. Wollen, co-founder of a home Bible study movement that spread through the United States, taught home Bible study seminars and worked with London pastors during the mission. Roberta addressed women's groups and motivated them to join the mission.

THE PALAU TEAM BOARD OF DIRECTORS

The Palau team's board of directors played vital roles in reaching London with the Gospel.

George Russell serves as the Luis Palau Evangelistic Team's chairman of the European board of directors. Russell also chairs Euroscot, a large meat import company. His background includes ten years as honorary organising secretary of Scottish Counties Evangelistic Movement. He lives in Glasgow with his wife, Moira. Russell was a member of the committee which brought Palau to preach in Scotland in 1981.

Duane Logsdon is the international chairman of the Luis Palau Evangelistic Team and president of Specialty Products Company, Santa Clara, California. The company designs and manufactures products for the plumbing industry. Logsdon and his wife Carole pastored four churches before devoting their time to their business.

Barrie Cirel from Cardiff, another member of the Luis Palau Evangelistic Team's European board of directors, gave his time and treasures to spread the Gospel in London. Cirel and his wife Brenda first met Palau in 1976, when they helped to coordinate a Welsh rally for the evangelist. During Mission to London, the Cirels spent most of their time in London for the crusade.

Dr Ted Engstrom, a member of the Palau team's North American board of directors, is also chief executive officer for World Vision/USA in California. While visiting the London crusade Engstrom said: 'The response to the Gospel in London is very readily received. And that's encouraging.'

Palau had been accused by some as not addressing social

needs, but Engstrom said: 'Luis has a very keen social
conscience. You can't separate from the New Testament the
social concern for the widow, the fatherless, the hungry or
the hurting. Luis has a deep concern for that, but the driving
force of his heart is evangelism. And what he is doing in
London is preaching the Gospel.'

MISSION TO LONDON STAFF

The Mission to London staff was a team of dedicated Christians. Peter Meadows had been involved in the mission since
its early planning stages. He said: 'Such a massive initiative in
evangelism is a once-in-a-generation opportunity and it must
be seized. You can't be complacent in a city where only four
per cent of the population actually attend a Protestant church
on a reasonably regular basis. For all of us involved with the
mission, our goal is that the mission should not only proclaim, but it also should be an instrument for change.'

David Austin, who left his long-time position with
London's police force to join the mission staff as area administrator and field supervisor, said: 'Something I've learned
from Luis is to think very positively, and dream big dreams
about what God can do in London through His church. Luis
doesn't talk negatively about the church's future in London.
He is always looking up, talking up, and thinking up. That's
a great strength.'

Alan Johnson, who joined the crusade staff in late 1983,
supervised the mission staff and controlled the office
finances, masterminding operations within the stadium.
After the mission he joined the Luis Palau team as the
European administrator.

Johnson, like so many others, often worked sixteen-hour
days during the mission. He said: 'When my prayer life and
walk with the Lord is right, the energy is just there. The Lord
provides.'

Julian Rowlandson, executive assistant of Mission to
London, described how the mission had proven to many
Christians the extent of the apathy in London's churches.

Rowlandson stressed that people didn't recognise their spiritual needs.

The Honourable Susie Sainsbury, chairman of the mission's women's committee, said: 'The exciting thing is the large percentage of people who are responding to the message and coming forward to receive Christ. That surely demonstrates the spiritual hunger in London.'

Cathie Smith, missions coordinator at Scripture Union, was chairman of the Mission to London children's committee, and for more than eighteen months organised specialised outreach to children.

John Hughes, central field supervisor, supervised approximately one thousand volunteers who spent many hours after each QPR meeting typing cards used to link each enquirer to a church. Many of these people also served as counsellors or stewards in addition to working regular day jobs.

Janet Morgan's role in the mission included organising the women's outreach, planning special children's events, and training children's counsellors. Morgan, a missionary supported by her church in America, said: 'By reaching out to children we're finding that we're reaching out to entire families. Non-Christian parents have come to know the Lord through outreach to their children.'

To motivate London churches' involvement in the mission Bill White, an area administrator, travelled in his area showing Luis Palau videos and talking to pastors. Soon the number of Christians White had spoken with about the mission grew from fifteen to thousands. When the mission ended, these Christians had distributed 30,000 invitations to QPR in White's area.

White saw many positive changes during the mission, but the most exciting for him was when his own daughter received Christ.

MTL COUNCIL, EXECUTIVE AND PROGRAMME COMMITTEES

Mission to London's council, executive and programme committees were composed of leaders in Christian service, government and business. The council consisted of Sir Cyril Black, Alan Dyer, Dr Michael Griffiths, Dr Brian Johanson, Rev. Gilbert Kirby, Sir Kirby Laing, David Pickford, David Saunderson, Rev. John Stott and Rev. Duncan Whyte.

The executive committee, chaired by the Rev. Gilbert Kirby, consisted of Rev. Lyndon Bowring, Rev. Clive Calver, Rev. Michael Cole, Alan Dyer, Brenda Forward, Rev. Rob Frost, Charles Green, George Hider, Sir Maurice Laing, Rev. Colin Matthews, David Pickford, Rev. Roy Pointer, George Russell and Harvey Thomas.

The programme committee consisted of Rev. Les Ball, Rev. Peter Batiste, Rev. Lyndon Bowring, John Brown, Gerald Coates, Rev. David Greenaway, Pastor Dennis Greenidge, Rev. Colin Matthews, Peter Meadows, Pastor Vernon Nelson, Susie Sainsbury, Cathie Smith and Harvey Thomas.

David Pickford, Mission to London chairman, is also chairman of Haslemere Estates, a property development company. Pickford enjoys working with young people, and is president of the London area Boys Brigade. He and his wife host 2,000 youths at the Christian youth centre on their farm each year.

He said: 'The mission's second phase has been an enormous task, mobilising so many people and trying to motivate churches which are dormant and just lacking in enthusiasm. One of our main jobs has been building up church people. Another of our main tasks was to make sure everyone in London has heard of Luis Palau, Mission to London, and QPR. Taxi drivers, coach drivers, businessmen, all now know what Luis Palau stands for – preaching the Gospel. At long last people in London are talking about Christianity quite openly.

'I think thousands will look back at the mission as a time

when God was brought to the notice of people, when people were born again, and people started talking again about Christianity.'

The Rev. Gilbert Kirby was also chairman of Movement for World Evangelization. His background is rich in Christian work: general secretary of Britain's Evangelical Alliance, principal of London Bible College, chairman of the European and Middle East Congress on Evangelism, member of the planning committee for the International Congress on World Evangelization, and chairman of the Filey Holiday Crusade.

Kirby said: 'We feel Luis is raised up by God. He is a youthful, dynamic man who understands the British scene. He obviously loves Britain, and he seems to be on the wavelength of the younger generation. God's blessing has rested upon his ministry and many of us felt he was God's man for this hour.

'At each stage the mission has been a bridge builder. It has been exciting to see people from different churches working together. There is a oneness – a unity of the spirit. If no other good came from Mission to London, it has done amazing good by bringing local Christians together.'

The Rev. Lyndon Bowring also chaired the special outreach committee. His background as chairman of Christian Action, Research, and Education (CARE), an organisation working towards higher quality of family and national life in Britain, helped to prepare him for his work with the mission.

Harvey Thomas served as the volunteer chairman of publicity and public relations. His credentials included working as a freelance public relations consultant, with the Conservative Party his major client, and fifteen years with the Billy Graham Evangelistic Association. He said: 'When Billy Graham introduced me to Luis in 1970, he said, "I believe God is giving to Luis Palau the burden of world evangelism that our team has carried since World War II." Billy was right. I think the Lord spoke to my heart then too.'

The Rev. Roy Pointer, church growth consultant for Britain's Bible Society, served as Operation Andrew chairman during phase one of the mission.

The Rev. Clive Calver, general secretary of Britain's Evangelical Alliance and former director of British Youth for Christ, said: 'Mission to London has to awaken the interest of evangelical churches to evangelism. This mission has started a snowball rolling downhill. It was used by God as a beginning, not as a conclusion.'

The Rev. Colin Matthews, a staff member of Scripture Union, had the enormous task of chairing the mission's counselling and follow-up committees. George Hider was the mission's visitation chairman. He was also youth secretary of London City Mission, where he worked for more than twenty years.

The Rev. Rob Frost, the Methodist Conference's first ordained evangelist in thirty years, said: 'Too often we think, pray and talk too small. When I first joined the executive I wondered if they were all mad because they were talking of filling QPR stadium and winning thousands for the Lord. At no time in my life had I met people with such vision. In recent years England has experienced a real decline in church membership and in spirituality. To see people who really take God at His Word and pray and expect mighty things to be done has influenced my life tremendously.'

Brenda Forward was also chairman of the London Baptist Association's evangelism committee. The London Baptist Association is a group of 270 Baptist churches which joined to encourage each other in extending Christ's Kingdom in London.

The Rev. Michael Cole was also chairman of the Mission to London prayer committee. Cole, vicar of All Saints at Woodford Wells in Essex, said Palau disarmed his critics because no offerings were taken at the meetings, and he did not play with emotions.

Dr Brian Johanson is minister at City Temple, a United Reformed Church in a location converged upon by 250,000 commuters daily. Several times during the mission Palau addressed large lunchtime crowds of commuters at City Temple.

Johanson said: 'There's been a steady trickle of new people to our church who have come to know the Lord through the

Mission to London meetings. Our regular Thursday lunch-time service added 20 or 30 per cent after the mission.'

London businessman David Saunderson, also involved in the mission's finance, said: 'I've been encouraged to see so many Christians working together.'

The Rev. John Stott, Rector Emeritus of All Souls Church, Langham Place, said: 'Luis is wonderfully faithful. He doesn't pull his punches, but preaches straight from the Bible. Many people today know nothing about the Bible, and he's wise to know about this ignorance.'

The Rev. Duncan Whyte, general secretary of London City Mission, commented: 'Luis's preaching is related to people's personal problems and he's showing the Christian answer to them. Mission to London has transformed hundreds, if not thousands, of lives.'

ASSOCIATE EVANGELISTS

Several associate evangelists who shared the Mission to London platform, especially during phase one, preached in schools, factories and offices.

Born and raised in East London, Doug Barnett has been a full-time evangelist since 1962. His Christian service includes organising the department of evangelism at Moorlands Bible College and serving as evangelist for Young Life and, more recently, the Saltmine Trust.

During Mission to London, Barnett served as an associate evangelist, preaching wherever he was invited to talk about Christ.

Associate evangelist Eric Delve first contemplated Christianity while attending Billy Graham's 1954 Harringay crusade. Delve, who was twelve at the time remembers: 'I'd never seen a preacher who said what he meant like Billy did. I watched Billy, responded, and eventually knew that was what God wanted me to do.'

Delve's background includes six years as national evangelist with British Youth for Christ. For Mission to London he spoke at four phase one area missions. 'Mission to London has shown that large numbers will be drawn to the Gospel when it is proclaimed in a language people understand, and in a cultural context in which they feel at home . . .'

A third associate evangelist was American-born Dr Bill Thomas, French field director for Overseas Crusades. Thomas had served as a missionary, pastor and evangelist in Zaire, Western Europe, India, the Caribbean, northern Europe and Scandinavia.

During phase one Thomas preached at area missions and at a Spanish church in London. During phase two he was an instructor for the Christian life and service classes to train counsellors.

Ian Leitch, an associate evangelist from Scotland, has an extensive background including co-founder of the Heralds Trust, a musical/evangelistic organisation based in Scotland. Leitch coordinated Palau's Lanarkshire crusade in 1980 and worked at Palau crusades in America, Glasgow and Leeds. During Mission to London he served as a master of ceremonies, song leader and evangelist. When Palau became ill on the first night he was to speak at the West London mission, he requested that Leitch speak for him.

Ian Coffey, another associate evangelist, is director of evangelism for the Saltmine Trust. His background includes staff member of Movement for World Evangelization and member of British Youth for Christ's national executive committee. During Mission to London, he served as a master of ceremonies and associate evangelist several times.

Norman Sinclair, British director of World Literature Crusade, served as an associate evangelist during phase two.

MUSICIANS

Musicians and artists who worked with Mission to London include mime artist Geoffrey Stevenson, musicians Marilyn Baker, Bryn Haworth, Garth Hewitt, Graham Kendrick, Isobel Lindsay, Barry McGuire, Betty Lou Mills, John Pantry, Dave Pope, Cliff Richard, Adrian Snell, Sheila Walsh, the London Gospel Community Choir, the Mizo

Choir, the Saltmine Band, New Beginnings, On Call and the Continental Orchestra and Singers.

Dave Pope, well-known British singer and evangelist, served as songleader and master of ceremonies.

In 1980 he formed the Saltmine Trust, whose ministry includes evangelistic missions and music ministry in Britain and overseas. The Saltmine Band served as musicians for the mission.

Pope, who has worked periodically with Palau since the mid-1970s, has great respect for the evangelist: 'In a nutshell, he scratches where people itch. He preaches in such a way that Joe Public can understand what he is all about. He's not preaching platitudes, theological nuances and niceties. It's down-to-earth preaching, relating the God of creation to the man in the street.'

Cliff Richard, a rock and roll musician for twenty-five years and a Christian for nineteen, performed at QPR and at Mission England. Cliff said: 'Our responsibility these days as Christians is to get across our message as often as we can . . .'

John Pantry first worked with Palau during the British Our God Reigns tour in 1980, then during crusades in Scotland and America. Sheila Walsh had also previously worked with Palau in Scotland.

CHRISTIAN LEADERS AND SUPPORTERS

Dr Bill Bright, founder of Campus Crusade for Christ, made a guest appearance at QPR, and said of Luis: 'God is using him to inspire and motivate people on a world scale. He has a ministry wherever he goes.'

Another Christian leader who came to the capital for Mission to London was Dr Joseph Aldrich, president of Multnomah School of the Bible in Portland, Oregon, from which Palau graduated in 1961. Aldrich, author of the book *Life-Style Evangelism*, was a guest speaker at the Luis Palau School of Evangelism, a two-day evangelism seminar in

London. He said: 'We need to teach people that evangelism
is a way of living rather than something that we do in
preparation for an event.'

VOLUMES OF VOLUNTEERS

Mission to London required thousands of volunteers to stuff
envelopes, sing in the choir, counsel enquirers and perform
a multitude of other tasks.

One man volunteered to spend two weeks of his annual
holiday working daily at the QPR office. An elderly woman
volunteered in the office every day for six weeks. Husband
and wife Bill and Ruth Oliver, both just a few days short of
their sixty-eighth birthdays during QPR, played important
roles as volunteers. This dedicated couple missed only a few
QPR meetings in all six weeks of the mission. Oliver spoke of
Palau's frank method of preaching: 'No minister here would
dare preach like that from the pulpit. His congregation would
walk out. But Luis can do it.'

Many Mission to London volunteers travelled long dis-
tances and paid expensive fares from their own pockets to
reach QPR. One dedicated choir member travelled thirty
miles nightly and paid more than £21 per week for six weeks.
Six to eight volunteers from the London branch of the
Christian Police Association provided free security for the
stadium each night.

A counselling volunteer said: 'Luis Palau has the gift to
trigger a decision in people. Sometimes the decision is not
simply a commitment to Christ, but people coming back to
Christ, people wanting to resolve problems that they've had
for years.'

One volunteer summarised the unity among the thousands
of London Christians: 'It's been very exciting working with
people from other parts of the church, finding our common
ground in Jesus.'

Chapter 8

MOVING MOUNTAINS WITH PRAYER

Through prayer, mountains are moved and people are transformed.

'If this mission is effective it will not be because of standing in a pulpit, but because we are down on our knees,' said one Mission to London leader.[1]

Evangelists throughout history testified to the power of prayer. Hudson Taylor: 'It is possible to move men, through God, by prayer alone.' Charles H. Spurgeon: 'We not only *ought* to pray more, but we *must*.' John Wesley: 'All God's works are done through believing prayer.' D. L. Moody: 'Every work of God can be traced to some kneeling form.'

The following letter exemplifies the thousands of lives changed by the power of prayer during Mission to London: 'I was on the verge of losing my daughter, but your ministry has restored her back to us. She was a lovely and obedient girl until she reached the magic age of eighteen. Then she went wild and cut herself off from our family. She started staying out later than usual, and even staying away for weekends. She was arrogant, rude, and refused to go to church.

'I became very distraught, but kept praying for her and asked God to make me the kind of mother He would have me be. I invited my daughter to Mission to London, and to my astonishment, she readily agreed to go. She even brought her friend and her friend's mum with us, and all three gave their lives to the Lord. Isn't that something? My daughter is not perfect, but she is a changed girl. This experience has strengthened my faith immensely. I can now say with more assurance that God does answer prayer.'

A woman who received Christ during Mission to London

had been the recipient of years of diligent prayers from her grandmother and her missionary aunt, who were thrilled that their prayers had been answered during the mission.

Powerful prayer is a prerequisite to revival. E. M. Bounds, the great prophet of prayer, said: 'Every revival of which we have any record has been bathed in prayer.'

Evan Roberts, leader of the last revival which swept through Wales, often prayed: 'Bend us. Bend the Church and save the world.'[2]

Samuel Stevenson said: 'Our forefathers wept and prayed and agonised before the Lord for sinners to be saved, and would not rest until they were slain by the Sword of the Word of God. That was the secret of their mighty success; when things were slack and would not move, they wrestled in prayer till God poured out His Spirit upon the people and sinners were converted.'[3]

WORLDWIDE PRAYER PARTNERS

Palau urged Christians world-wide to wrestle in prayer for Mission to London: 'Before we talk to London about God, we must talk to God about London.'

Christians world-wide – including those in Sweden, the Netherlands, Guatemala, Peru, Mexico, Argentina and the United States – uplifted Mission to London in prayer.

Intercessors for Britain often prayed with other prayer groups for the mission.

The Lausanne Committee for World Evangelization listed the mission in its prayer calendar during phase one: 'Pray for an impact on this city that will affect many nations for the glory of God.'[4]

Crusade for World Revival requested prayer for the mission in their magazine *Revival* as early as November 1982, and continued requesting prayer for the mission throughout the crusade. Their prayer chain of 8,000 lifted up prayers for Mission to London as far away as Australia, Singapore and India.

PRAYER STRATEGIES

Revival reported of the prayer efforts of Mission to London:
'Under the dynamic leadership of Rev. Michael Cole, vicar of
All Saints, Woodford Wells, Essex, a prayer committee
comprising of Christians with powerful prayer lives has been
recruiting many prayer partners and linking up with various
prayer chains. Prayer groups have been springing up all over
London.'[5]

The prayer committee met monthly, and more frequently
as the central mission drew nearer. The majority of the
meeting time was spent not on discussion and planning, but
in earnest intercession.

Powerful intercession for the mission was aided by a
twenty-four-hour prayer hotline and various prayer structures. One of these structures was prayer triplets, in which
each individual prays regularly with two other Christians.
After each shares the names of three friends with spiritual
needs, the group prays for these nine friends, Mission to
London, Luis Palau, Mission England, Billy Graham and
one another. The triplets met at work, home, school or
church. Long prayer sessions were not a necessity, but
regular sessions were. Churches were united in reaching out
to their city when members of prayer triplets belonged to
different churches.

Prayer triplet groups were also encouraged to be Operation
Andrew partners with each other. In this programme, Christians pray for one or more unsaved people, build relationships with them and invite them to attend the mission
meetings.

London Christians were also encouraged to meet in small
prayer groups of two to six people before and during the
mission. These small groups took many forms – from coffee
mornings in homes, to businessmen's lunchtime meetings in
offices, to student Christian Union meetings on campuses.

The disabled, elderly and other immobile Christians unable to attend meetings can offer a most valuable ministry –
prayer. Mission to London was eager to tap the powerful

prayer lives of these Christians by asking them to be Mission to London home prayer partners.

The first of January 1984 was proclaimed a national day of prayer as a cooperative effort between Mission to London and Mission England. For several months prior to the crusade, two days per month were set aside as days of prayer for the mission. A month before the mission began, this doubled to four days per month. A month before the central meetings began, weekly lunchtime prayer meetings were hosted by four London churches: Westminster Chapel, Kensington Temple, All Souls Church and St Peter's Cornhill. Westminster Hall was the site for a women's day of prayer service. Other Greater London churches organised additional Mission to London prayer meetings which ranged from prayer breakfasts to all-night prayer sessions.

The Rev. Les Ball, Operation Andrew chairman and vicar at Clapham Park Baptist Church, spoke of the mission's beneficial prayer schemes: 'Prayer for our friends and neighbours to come to Christ had always been vague. Operation Andrew made it specific. Many prayer cells were formed to pray for unconverted friends. Praying for specific people has now become part of our lives and still continues.'

Palau wrote to the prayer committee chairman: 'I hear such good things about the prayer going up to God . . . I've heard about what some young people now call "Joshua Walks" around London. I understand that a group of godly Londoners have walked around the city praying for God to pour out His Spirit there. What an exciting prospect. I've been sharing this with other believers, and it's stirring prayer for London.'

Monthly prayer bulletins written jointly by Luis and Pat Palau were sent to 75,000 Christians across America to motivate them to pray fervently for Mission to London. When 8,000 Londoners had registered public Christian commitments by the end of the campaign's first phase, Mrs Palau wrote: 'Our Father, how can we adequately praise You for the thousands of lives You changed this autumn in London? Thank You for allowing us to have a part in this spiritual harvest. Millions in London still need to know You, Lord.

Help Luis and the team members as they return to London this summer to proclaim the Gospel again.

'Lord, You know the tremendous spiritual needs in Britain. Bind the power of Satan and guide the preparations for the second phase of Mission to London. May multiplied thousands hear the Gospel of Jesus Christ and commit their lives to you. Where there is despair, show Your way. Where there is unbelief, proclaim Your truth. Where there is emptiness, bestow Your abundant life. O Lord, revive Britain again.'

As the second phase of the mission grew nearer, tremendous prayer support grew daily. A week before the mission began, Palau prayed with his team and international supporters: 'O Lord, pour out Your Holy Spirit on London and all of Britain today. Pour out Your Spirit on Billy Graham today as he preaches in England. We pray that thousands of British men and women will come to Christ through Mission to London and Mission England. May we see a mighty unleashing of Your power in London this summer.

'Lord, put to flight the forces of darkness. Draw the attention of the mass media. Turn on, we pray, the light in England, and give us a mighty harvest. Bring revival to the British Isles, and bless us and use us to Your glory. Amen.'

The renewed interest in prayer did not end with the mission. On 12 January, 1985 – six months after the mission ended – 4,500 people gathered in the Royal Albert Hall for 'Pray for London', an evening of prayer organised by Mission to London. Almost one thousand people were unable to obtain tickets for the event, which is believed to be Britain's largest prayer meeting in thirty years.

Chapter 9

BIDDING THEM COME

The basic structure for Mission to London was set. Thousands of British Christians were planning, preparing and praying for the campaign. But another essential task – bringing unbelievers to the meetings to hear the Gospel – lay ahead. This was achieved via three major outreaches to London's non-Christians: Operation Andrew, visitation and saturation evangelism.

OPERATION ANDREW

Operation Andrew was the central method of bringing the unconverted and unchurched to Mission to London to hear the Gospel. The term is based on John 1:42: 'Andrew brought Simon to Jesus.'

Each 'Andrew' prayed for one or more uncommitted friends, developed their friendship, and brought them to the mission with his church's Operation Andrew group.

Operation Andrew had five steps: Pray daily for friends and family with spiritual needs; develop friendships with them; bring them to Mission to London to hear the Gospel; encourage them to commit their lives to Christ; and follow them up in the church.

Each Andrew listed the names of unsaved friends on his Operation Andrew card, which reminded him to pray for his friends and to invite them to the mission. Andrews were also encouraged to pray for their unsaved friends with a partner or in groups.

An Operation Andrew pamphlet produced by Mission to London said of Andrew: 'He wasn't a preacher; in fact the Bible shows there was nothing special about him at all. But Andrew was a very special link in God's chain. After John the Baptist introduced Andrew to Jesus, we read "he brought Simon to Jesus" (John 1:42). We all know how important Simon Peter was to become in God's plan; how wonderful that the Andrew link didn't fail.

'Andrew was a bringer. He brought his brother Simon to meet Jesus. When some Greeks wanted to meet Jesus, it was Andrew who brought them together. Not many of us are called to be a Peter or a Paul, but we can all be Andrews. We can all be bringers.'

The Rev. Norman Warren, Rector of Morden, and Wimbledon mission chairman, said: 'The Operation Andrew scheme has been one of the very great strengths of this mission. In our church and many other churches, those who were converted even before the mission began were those being prayed for in the Operation Andrew plan.'

Thousands of Londoners were introduced to Christ through the mission's Operation Andrew plan. One couple prayed for a backslidden Christian friend and his unsaved wife, invited them to their home for dinner and took them to QPR afterwards. There the husband rededicated his life to Christ and his wife was converted.

A man added his cousin to his Operation Andrew list and began praying that she would attend Mission to London. Both times he asked his cousin to the mission she refused to come, but he continued praying for her. The third time he invited her, not only did she agree to come, but she also brought her husband. Both were converted that night. The woman later said that her cousin's persistence showed that he really cared for her.

One woman listed the members of her neighbourhood Bible study group on her Operation Andrew card. She began praying for her neighbours, and invited them to the mission, where three received Christ.

A Mission to London volunteer added a family of three to his Operation Andrew list, prayed for them, and invited them to the southeast London mission. But the tent was damaged by a gale and that night's meeting was cancelled. So the volunteer invited the family to tea instead. As they enjoyed biscuits and tea, the volunteer explained the Gospel and led all three to Christ.

VISITATION

George Hider was responsible for involving London Christians in inviting unbelievers to the mission.

The first phase of the visitation began in March 1983, when London Christians distributed 100,000 copies of *Luke for London*, a booklet including Luke's Gospel and a message from Luis Palau. Hider described these booklets as 'excellent evangelistic tools for visitation'. Londoners were encouraged to give the booklets to their friends and neighbours when they invited them to Mission to London. In 1984, 50,000 copies were distributed. Hider said: 'It was very encouraging that many churches and individuals who hadn't done door-to-door visitation previously started doing it because of *Luke for London*.' Hider also supervised each area mission's visitation plans, which were divided into smaller areas for specific churches to visit.

Hider added: 'One outstanding church, Clapham Park Baptist Church, visited 11,000 homes and distributed 700 copies of *Luke for London* during phase one, which was quite tremendous. That church has seen some of the best results in the way of referrals and new converts.'

The final wave of visitation began in May 1984, prior to the meetings at QPR stadium. The phase two strategy included plans to visit four million homes with an invitation to join the local church's Andrew groups going to QPR. Each church within forty miles of London had been encouraged to visit all homes within a half-mile radius. Although the goal was not completely fulfilled, intensive visitation took place in every London postal district. This was supported by teams of young people coordinated by Operation Mobilisation and the London City Mission.

When one Christian visitor knocked on an elderly couple's door, the couple planned to get rid of whoever was calling upon them. But the Lord had other plans. Instead of throwing their visitor out, the couple asked the Christian into their home and they invited Christ into their hearts.

The Rev. Norman Warren, an area mission chairman, said: 'In our own church about sixty people were trained and involved in the door-to-door visitation. This was a new experience for them, but they're clammering to do this again. There has been a new incentive to get out of the walls of the church and get into the homes in the parish. They have been surprised by the welcome they have received in so many homes.'

SATURATION EVANGELISM

For six weeks in June and July 1984 a team of approximately twenty-five Christians saturated 60,000 homes in a two-mile radius of QPR with invitations to Mission to London.

American Bill MacLeod, who supervised this saturation evangelism team, explained: 'This was not an exercise in leaflet door-stuffing, but an opportunity to engage in conversation and personally invite residents to come to the mission meetings. The Gospel was shared as team members went door-to-door through neighbourhoods.'

MacLeod contacted more than one hundred churches within a two-mile radius of QPR stadium, personally meeting with each minister and challenging them to do evangelism in their churches. Only fifteen actively participated in the mission, and only eleven worked with the saturation evangelism team. MacLeod said: 'The minority of the churches did the majority of the work.'

The 40 members of the saturation evangelism team had little or no previous experience in saturation evangelism. The team's diverse background included several students, teachers, church workers, a dentist, a truck driver, an accountant, a professional actor, and a computer programmer. They were volunteers who paid their own expenses with the help of their home churches. The group had members from the United States, Finland, Africa, Australia, England, Wales and Scotland. MacLeod said: 'God has moved around the world to bring people here to be part of this team.'

The daily goal was to saturate an area with more than 2,000 personal invitations to the mission, yet without resorting to simply stuffing leaflets through doors. In the six-week period, the team covered more than 600 streets, visited 58,200 homes, distributed 69,800 invitations to QPR and more than 57,000 additional pieces of literature, including evangelistic tracts, the Gospel of Luke, and the guest passes to QPR. They visited an average of 2,300 homes daily.

Under the direction of Colin Wolrich, a professional actor and dedicated Christian, some members rode the underground trains and in a short, positive announcement invited people to the meetings and distributed leaflets to each commuter. An additional 106,000 invitations were distributed outside central underground stations near the stadium.

Distributing invitations to QPR was more difficult in the area's pockets of diverse cultures. Many people they encountered were Iranian, Iraqi and Indian, and spoke little or no English. But God overcame cultural barriers to see that the Gospel was proclaimed. At least ten thousand invitation leaflets were distributed in the Shepherd's Bush market one Saturday.

A Hindu girl prayed to receive Christ with a team member who came to her door to invite her to QPR. One morning a team member took a Gospel written in an Eastern language he didn't understand. A man he met that day didn't understand English, but was pleased to receive the foreign tract, which was in his native tongue.

Joseph Sakyi-Mante, a computer programmer from Ghana, had worked as a missionary in Malaysia and Singapore with the Haggai Institute before joining the saturation evangelism team. While distributing Mission to London literature in a market district, Sakyi-Mante entered a butcher's shop and asked the butcher if he could leave some literature for his customers. Although the butcher was an Arab Muslim, he cleared a place on his counter for the tracts.

Rich Flashman, a student at Trinity Evangelical Divinity School in the United States, was deeply moved when a seventy-year-old blind woman prayed to receive Christ when Flashman came to her door to invite her to Mission to London.

One team member – a sixty-two-year-old Scotsman – met a woman he had known in Bible class in Glasgow twenty years earlier. Although she was not involved in a church, she was open to hearing her old friend discuss Mission to London.

MacLeod said, 'We've been encouraging each other that when we go out, we're really just keeping divine appointments that God has made for us. God has put us there to meet these people. We made the plans, but we must be on God's schedule.'

Justice Arhinful, a Ghanaian missionary to Nigeria, had ministered in Nigeria for nine years, had a church of 600, and was supervising ten other Nigerian churches when he heard about the short-term saturation evangelism opportunity with Mission to London. He said: 'I came to assist the work here, to see that souls are being saved to the glory of God. My vision for the work in Africa has expanded, and especially the vision I have for my own country, Ghana.'

MacLeod said: 'We are blessing the nations by doing what God has led us to do here in London because now team members want to take these techniques home with them to their countries.'

A British accountant said: 'I led a fifty-three-year-old to the Lord, and witnessed his baptism a month later.' An American student said: 'Seeing hundreds come to Christ at QPR each night made the daytime tiredness easier to bear. I feel I have grown spiritually from being on the team.' A London minister said: 'I've learned to live a life of witnessing rather than be a witness in specific times.' A Scottish graduate student remarked: 'I learned to pray for revival.' A London curate said: 'It has changed my life, and has been the third most important event in my Christian life. I am more keen on evangelism now.' A Finnish student commented: 'It has been great to see how God is working within the mass of people, yet to God we are still so important as individuals.'

MacLeod said: 'The individuals who took part and the churches who backed the mission were the most blessed. Not only have they touched an area with the Gospel, but in the process their lives have been so marked by the Gospel that each has returned to his home equipped and desiring to carry out the same work there.'

Chapter 10

THE MISSION AND THE MEDIA

Mission to London received more publicity than any previous Palau crusade. In addition to the media coverage, the £300,000 advertising campaign by the Sales Promotion Agency, a subsidiary of Saatchi & Saatchi, also reminded Londoners everywhere they went – including the underground trains – that something significant was happening at QPR stadium.

Tom Davies reported in the *Sunday Express Magazine*: 'Mission to London wants everyone in the city to have heard of Palau by the time he leaves.'[1]

That goal was achieved, as *Punch* reported: 'One can hardly move around the City at the moment without being collared by bright-eyed strangers who try to persuade you that life cannot be worth living until one has heard the preachings of this evangelistic chappie, Luis Palau.'[2]

THE METHOD

Some journalists didn't conceal their cynicism about mass evangelism. One wrote: 'If you can spare two hours to devote to your redemption, Palau's your man.'[3]

But when a minority of Methodist clergymen gained media attention for calling crusade evangelism 'crude', Graham Jones reported Palau's response in the *Daily Telegraph*: 'I do not think it is any cruder than John or Charles Wesley in their day when they stood on street corners and were pelted with rotten eggs when they preached the Gospel. If preaching to the masses is considered crude, then I welcome the insult.'[4]

Many journalists were surprised at the lack of emotional-ism at QPR. One wrote that when Palau spoke at QPR: 'There was no hysteria, and certainly he did not play upon our emotions.' He added that there was 'no whipping up of enthusiasm . . . What happened next quite took me by surprise, for they went out across the stadium in the hundreds, not to meet Luis, not to meet people, but to come into a new and living relationship with the Lord Jesus Christ.'[5]

THE MESSAGE

Palau's simple but powerful Gospel message grabbed the media's attention.

Martyn Halsall wrote in the *Baptist Times*: 'Luis Palau fashions his sermons with a blowtorch and delivers them while still white-hot.'[6]

Halsall wrote in the *Guardian* that Palau 'proclaimed forgiveness, through faith in Christ's death and resurrection, with arms outstretched: a distant, dark-suited figure in a pool of floodlighting'.[7]

'Palau's gospel isn't a weak-kneed antidote to the free-living spirit of the eighties,' wrote Garry Jenkins in the *Guardian*. 'His message is hard-hitting, and it sticks.'[8]

Veronica Horwell observed in the *Sunday Times*: 'His words were not smooth' and his message was 'like bitter chocolate'.[9]

In the *Catholic Herald* Gerard Noel wrote that Palau's message contains 'in ultimate logic, the implication that an awful lot of people go to hell'.[10]

The *Church of England Newspaper* highlighted Mission to London throughout the campaign, and reported the over-whelming success of Mission to London and Billy Graham's Mission England: 'It is heartening to note that the orthodox traditional Christian message still has power to change minds and hearts.'[11]

When John Cunningham of the *Guardian* asked Palau if his

message would be updated for London, he repeated the evangelist's reply: 'It's a proclamation which does not change. What empties the churches is when you do change it.'[12]

Some journalists even allowed Palau to freely discuss the Gospel and its potential impact upon London. Reviewing a BBC1 *Everyman* programme which spotlighted Mission to London, the *Church of England Newspaper* wrote: 'Luis Palau could hardly hope for a better chance to present the Gospel in the course of a television interview than the one afforded to him by that excellent reporter, Peter France, in *Everyman: Hell to Pay*.' The review concluded: 'I don't think I have ever seen the case for biblical Christianity put more clearly or more convincingly on television.'[13]

In the *Daily Mirror* William Marshall wrote of Palau: 'He exudes honesty and sincerity like a burst water main.'[14]

THE UNITY

In the *Ealing Gazette* a Roman Catholic layman reminded readers of the uncommon unity among churches supporting the mission: 'Over 1,700 churches in the London area of all denominations have been preparing for the last eighteen months for this evangelical mission at QPR. Luis Palau's arrival during June is merely the climax of much hard ground work already undertaken by many Christians.'[15]

Under the headline 'We'll feel the effects for years', the *Baptist Times* notes three reasons for the long-term success of the Graham and Palau missions: the 'unexpectedly high' responses at the meetings, the 'thorough' and 'effective' follow-up by local churches, and the 'impressive' level of cooperation among the churches.[16]

Noting the 'startling' response rate at QPR, the *Church Times* reported: 'The seeds cast forth fell on well-prepared ground: evidently long hours of prayer, careful invitation, consistent friendship, and persuasion.'[17]

THE IMPACT

The second phase of Mission to London appeared in at least two hundred articles in Britain's secular and Christian press, in addition to scores of radio and television newscasts.

At his last London press conference, Palau said: 'I think honestly that the journalists of Britain have wished us success.'

In addition to excellent media coverage in Britain, Mission to London also received world-wide coverage, appearing in publications in the United States, Australia, the Caribbean, Africa and elsewhere.

Ray Hosking wrote in *Impact*, an Australian publication: 'London's church leaders are praying that this year's mission will not only encourage church growth, but will ignite a full-scale religious revival throughout the city.'[18]

Referring to the impact of Mission to London and two other evangelistic programmes, London's *Sunday Express Magazine* wrote of the British church: 'This ailing old institution is never going to be the same again.'[19]

SECTION THREE

PHASE ONE –
THE AREA MISSIONS

Chapter 11

THE BEGINNING – TRAFALGAR SQUARE

'This rally is symbolic of what the Lord Jesus Christ wants to do here in London,' Luis Palau told 8,000 Christians jammed into Trafalgar Square. 'I believe that the Lord has raised up the British Isles to spread the Gospel to all the world.'

This 3 September 1983 dedication rally marked the commencement of Mission to London's first phase – the area missions.

Palau compared the Gospel to the Battle of Trafalgar and Admiral Lord Nelson, whose monument stands in Trafalgar Square: 'It reminds me of our Lord Jesus Christ, who won a great victory on the cross of Calvary, and He, too, gave His life in that victory. But the difference is that Jesus is alive today.

'As we minister in London and as our beloved brother Billy Graham visits other major cities in England, how exciting it will be over the next ten months as we raise the flag of the cross and say to all the United Kingdom, "Jesus is alive today."'

An hour before the rally Palau, his team members and mission administrators had gathered to pray fervently in St Martins Church across the street from the square. As they were praying, the crowd in the square continued to grow, undaunted by the rain.

Colourful banners bearing names of churches of many denominations bobbed in the square, testifying to the unity among hundreds of London churches: Holy Trinity Brompton, St Peter's Edgware, Tottenham Corner Free Church, Clapham Park Baptist Church, Camden Town

Methodist Church, Gainsborough Gospel, Southgate Christian Fellowship and Salway Evangelical Church. At the rally, churches exchanged banners with one another and prayed for each other throughout Mission to London.

Policemen stood at the outer edge of the square to keep an eye on what proved to be a most cooperative crowd. From the red double-decker buses passing through the square, passengers peered to find out what was happening in Trafalgar Square. Journalists crowded around and upon Nelson's column.

Then the crowd broke into small groups to pray for the mission, for Palau, for the associate evangelists and for London. The Rev. Michael Cole led in prayer.

Addressing the crowd a second time, Palau spoke of the dedication of Britain's new spiritual leadership: 'They are young men and women who have the fire of the power of the Holy Spirit upon them.' He challenged these young leaders: 'Don't let that fire die out. Be filled with the Holy Spirit. Be filled with the fire of God. The fire must be proclaimed to this generation of young people.

'My beloved friends, work, work, work for Christ. Witness for Christ. Work, for the night is coming.'

With these words phase one of Mission to London began. These grass-roots area missions provided an opportunity to take the Gospel to the masses in many of London's boroughs, and to touch the lives of thousands with Jesus Christ.

Chapter 12

THE GRASS-ROOTS AREA MISSIONS

From the opening of the Ilford mission in late August to the close of the Wembley meetings in late October, more than 210,000 people attended the phase one area missions, and 8,000 made decisions for Christ.

The lives of these 8,000 people were dramatically changed by Jesus Christ, as this letter reveals: 'When my husband, our two children and I went to the Big Top on Clapham Common, we all went forward to give our lives to the Lord Jesus Christ. I cannot adequately express my feelings. My husband is an alcoholic – but the Lord be praised – he has not had a drink since then. I am eternally grateful. God bless you.'

A couple who believed their marriage was beyond hope had decided to get a divorce. A few days before they were to send their divorce papers to the solicitor, they came to the Ilford mission separately, without knowing the other had come. Both came forward at Eric Delve's invitation to receive Christ. Seeing each other at the front of the tent, they held hands, knelt together on the tent's muddy ground, and committed their lives to Christ. Then they went home together and tore up their divorce papers. When their sixteen-year-old daughter saw how Christ had changed her parents' lives and saved their marriage, she came to the crusade the next night and gave her life to Christ too.

A husband whose wife was converted at the earlier mission at Highbury went forward at the Newham mission and received Christ.

At Clapham a woman accepted the Lord one night, and the

next day she brought her husband to the counselling centre, and he also gave his life to Christ.

A man who refused to make a commitment to Christ at the Wimbledon mission could not sleep. In his distress, he got out of bed and visited the couple who had brought him to the meeting. In the early morning hours he received Christ as his Saviour.

Two sisters, one Christian and one non-Christian, rode a coach to the Clapham mission to hear Luis Palau preach. At the meeting the unsaved sister gave her life to Christ. When both sisters remained after the meeting to talk with a counsellor, their coach left without them, and they had to take a taxi home. Instead of being angry about the coach leaving without her, the new Christian was so full of joy that she told their taxi driver how she had met Jesus Christ in the tent on Clapham Common that very night. The driver was so interested in what she told him about the Gospel that he came to the crusade the following night and gave his life to Christ too.

Another Londoner writes: 'I was saved eight months ago at your meeting on Clapham Common. Since then, Christ has completely transformed my life. Praise the Lord, and thank you, Luis.'

Another letter reads: 'When I became a Christian four years ago I began praying for my husband's salvation. My husband and I attended the Croydon mission meeting, and although he did not go forward at the invitation, he was interested in Luis's message. The next night he returned to the mission alone and went forward to give his life to Christ. I can't express the joy we felt that night as we prayed together for the first time in our eight years of marriage.

'Our life has changed. Now we take our problems to Christ together. Our children have noticed the difference in their father and our home. Our church elders have prayed weekly for my husband's conversion for the past two years. What happiness in seeing their prayers answered!'

A THOUSAND CHURCHES STRONG

Mission to London was truly a people's mission. Each of the nine area missions was responsible for setting its budget and raising the needed funds from local Christians.

The Rev. Norman Warren said: 'We felt very strongly in the area of finances. We wanted to have every penny before the mission. We didn't want to mention money at the meetings. Non-Christians are very sensitive about this – that Christians are after their money. We wanted people to hear the free gift of salvation in Christ without any mention of money.'

Gordon Thornton, the Blackheath mission administrator, was impressed by the unity among the churches preparing for the mission: 'For the first time in my experience, Christians of all denominations have worked together, sat on committees together, prayed together and worshipped together. The unity displayed has been a tremendous inspiration.'

The Rev. Clive Calver said that Mission to London was 'different in the variety of regional missions and, therefore, in the variety of churches and individuals involved. It's very encouraging to see the way that the mission has gone into local areas – often depressed areas – and given an opportunity for churches to mobilise and encourage each other and be committed to each other.'

The Rev. Bill Thomas said: 'Mission to London was a great experience for me. It was the first time I've been involved in what I would call a well-prepared, area-wide crusade.'

Thomas said that because most evangelistic campaigns in London's recent past have been located in one central stadium, 'churches haven't had to be as fully involved and committed as they have been in the area-wide crusades, where everything is on a smaller scale.'

The Rev. Norman Warren, Wimbledon mission chairman, said: 'In Wimbledon more than two hundred churches are working together in an amazing way which I think will continue. We've seen a new desire to evangelise the area, a new expectancy among the ministers in the power of the simple Gospel to bring people to faith in Christ.'

The Rev. Les Ball, Clapham mission chairman and minister at Clapham Park Baptist Church, Bonneville, said: 'Mission to London made us focus much more sharply on how committed we really were to evangelism. It challenged us and exposed how much lip service we pay to evangelism in contrast to our actual involvement. We were challenged as individuals and as a church to not only take evangelism seriously, but also to take it personally. Many members were encouraged by being part of something big that God was doing. Everyone felt useful.'

The Rev. Dennis Peterson of St Jude's, an Anglican church in Brixton, said: 'Many churches in Greater London are pitifully small and weak. Yet our congregation has been greatly encouraged by the mission and has experienced an awakening of the responsibility of witness. The church has been lifted on to a new level of concern for evangelism.'

The Rev. Thomas Lynds of St Luke's, an Anglican church in Wimbledon, said the mission helped 'increase an awareness of the great needs of the people and to face up to the many problems of presenting the Gospel today'.

Since the Wimbledon mission, Lynds has noted spiritual growth in his congregation and 'a greater freedom in speaking of things of God'. His congregation is 'seeking to reach those who have no contact with our Lord Jesus Christ'.

The Rev. Geoffrey Birch, Croydon mission follow-up chairman, said: 'I hear many reports of baptismal services and new believers being added to the church. All of us involved in the Croydon crusade praise the Lord for what He has done.'

The Rev. Charles Hutchins, Blackheath mission chairman, said: 'Local churches should be mobilised to reach out in confidence to their communities. In many areas this has happened with exciting results.'

THE AREA MISSIONS

Palau spoke at nine Greater London area missions: east, Ilford; inner north, Highbury; inner south, Clapham; west, Hounslow; inner east, Newham; northeast, Walthamstow; southeast, Blackheath; south, Croydon; and southwest, Wimbledon.

The first area mission was in Valentines Park, Ilford, where Eric Delve addressed the majority of the meetings. By the last night, when Palau spoke in the 1,500-capacity tent, the crowds from the tent and a smaller overflow tent spilled on to the grass surrounding the big tent.

From Ilford, Palau travelled to London's inner north to preach in a 3,500-seat tent at Highbury Field, where Bill Thomas preached the first week. Palau preached the remaining five days.

The third mission was on Clapham Common. Associate evangelists including Eric Delve and Doug Barnett spoke on the first twelve days of the mission, and Palau preached the last five days. The 3,500-capacity tent was visited by more than 24,000 people, and more than 700 of these made public decisions for Christ.

Clapham Common has been the site of other mass evangelism campaigns. Charles Spurgeon lived there and sometimes preached on the Common. D. L. Moody also preached there during his London campaign in the nineteenth century.

The longest area mission, the seventeen-day campaign on Hounslow Heath, attracted almost thirty-one thousand people. Of these, 946 made public Christian commitments, and many exciting testimonies emerged. One coach brought sixty people from Maidenhead to the Hounslow mission, and at the invitation, twenty-four of them gave their lives to Christ.

The northeast London mission in a large tent in Walthamstow was attended by more than 13,500 people, with 577 of these making public decisions for Christ.

Canon Harry Sutton, Walthamstow mission administrator, told how a young couple was transformed at the mission there. The wife, a nominal Christian, rededicated her life to the Lord at the women's meeting. That night she brought her husband to the crusade meeting, and he accepted Christ.

Sutton said: 'That's the kind of thing that has been happening here in Walthamstow and we rejoice.'

On the last night of the mission there he said: 'We are going home tonight praising God that in spite of the opposition, in spite of the other voices that cry out for the souls of northeast London, the voice of Christ has been clearly heard by the thousands who have packed this tent every night.

'This may be the last night of the crusade, but it's not the last night of the battle. We are going to prepare, reorganise our forces, marshal our resources, learn from the past and go forward into the future in a new and vital way.'

From Walthamstow, Palau travelled to another tent mission – this one in Newham's Baalam Street Park. During this short mission, which was supported by approximately thirty-five area churches, more than six thousand people heard the Gospel. Although Palau preached in Newham for only two days, Doug Barnett, the Saltmine Band and a British Youth for Christ team were involved in many facets of evangelism in the inner east.

Barnett spoke about mass evangelism in the Newham area: 'For so long folk have said, "This is the East End. Things don't happen here" – as if God stopped at Tower Bridge and never turned right to come down Commercial Road. I don't believe that for one minute. I believe God has always been at work here. And now we're going to see the breakthrough in a small way. The small streams of blessing are beginning to come, and I believe it will grow into a mighty river in the days to come.'

Barnett says the area has a 'fairly heavy interest in what could generally be termed "occult" things' which has 'made life tough for some of the Christians in the borough. You're battling with the forces of darkness in a very real sense here. But God has done some remarkable things.'

Drawn by curiosity, one man wandered into the Newham tent before the meeting began one evening to find out what was happening there. He was counselled and received the Lord on the spot.

A Christian man whose family opposed Christianity persuaded his mother to attend the Newham mission, and at the invitation, she went forward to give her life to Christ, as her son watched, weeping with joy.

Palau was the sole evangelist to speak at the five-day Croydon mission in Fairfield Halls, the same site where D. L. Moody had preached during his Mission to London a century earlier. More than eleven thousand people attended Palau's Croydon mission, which was supported by more than one hundred and thirty area churches.

As in Moody's mission, hundreds of lives were changed by the power of Christ at Croydon. A local headmaster who was also an ordained minister saw two of his daughters give their lives to Christ at a mission meeting. A retired couple came forward hand-in-hand at the appeal and rededicated their lives to the Lord.

A week before the mission a youth evangelist spoke at a Croydon school and offered an invitation to receive Christ. That night a boy in the class died, causing many of his classmates to think about life after death. This boy's best friend asked a Christian master how to become a Christian and received Christ. The following week coachloads of boys attended the Croydon mission and twenty-seven received Christ. Soon afterwards when a Church Army team spoke in this school a dozen more boys became Christians. Now the school's chaplain and Christian teachers have organised nurture groups and Bible studies, which have become quite popular with the boys.

The southwest London mission in Wimbledon Theatre was attended by almost twelve thousand people in five days. Although the theatre seats only 2,000, overflow sites at a nearby church and town hall increased the maximum seating capacity to more than three thousand.

The approximately two hundred area churches supporting the Wimbledon mission witnessed hundreds of lives changed by Christ. For twenty years a Christian husband prayed daily that his wife would return to the Lord. Much to his surprise, his wife agreed to come to the Wimbledon mission, where she rededicated her life to the Lord. Now she regularly attends church with her husband, who is thrilled that God answered his prayers.

Southeast London's mission in a 3,000-seat tent erected at Blackheath attracted 30,700 people. More than one thousand made public Christian commitments there.

A day before Palau was to preach there, colossal winds ripped fourteen-foot gashes in the tent's roof and bent the steel poles anchoring the gigantic structure. That night's meeting was cancelled. Volunteers were recruited to quickly dismantle the electronic and lighting equipment and 2,500 folding chairs.

The next night the tent was still being repaired, so the meeting was relocated to a church in nearby Greenwich. The sudden relocation did not hinder 2,200 people from gathering to hear Palau preach the Gospel. The next day the winds had subsided and the repaired tent was erected in time for the 7 p.m. service which was attended by 3,500 people eager to hear the Gospel.

Like Clapham Common and Croydon's Fairfield Halls, Blackheath has also played a part in London's rich Christian heritage. During the Great Awakening, George Whitefield preached to massive crowds at Blackheath several times. During Mission to London, Blackheath was once again the site of a great spiritual harvest, with hundreds taking the step towards changed lives by receiving Christ as Lord and Saviour in the tent on the heath.

A spiritualist medium who attended the Blackheath mission came forward at the invitation and gave her life to Christ.

The night a tough gang leader attended the mission, blind musician Marilyn Baker shared her testimony and sang before Palau preached. Deeply touched by Marilyn's testimony, the gang leader wandered into the Mission's family counselling centre, where he committed his life to Jesus Christ. The youth stepped forward at the appeal to publicly express his decision.

THE MARC EUROPE FOLLOW-UP STUDY

Six months after the area missions had ended, Peter Brierley of Missions Advanced Research and Communications Centre in Britain (MARC Europe) completed an extensive study of the phase one missions.

Total decisions during Mission to London phase one were 3·9 per cent of the attendance – comparable to the results of previous Luis Palau and Billy Graham campaigns. The lengthy Clapham mission had the smallest percentage of enquirers – only 2·9 per cent. But the much shorter, five-day Wimbledon mission had the largest percentage of enquirers, with a surprising 7 per cent of those attending making public decisions for Christ.

The Rev. Norman Warren, Wimbledon mission chairman, said: 'The large number coming forward at the meetings was more than I was honestly expecting because Londoners don't readily commit themselves. The way that Luis seemed to be on the wavelength of Londoners, and the attentive audiences during his hour-long sermons, were indications that he was smack on the mark.'

The Rev. Bob Groves, vicar of All Saints, Clapham Park, echoed the enthusiasm of hundreds of church leaders involved in the mission: 'How exciting these missions have been!' Groves reports that his church has 'more than doubled' since the beginning of their commitment to Mission to London.

Mission to London's area campaigns changed individual lives, families and churches. Could they together change London?

Gordon Thornton, Blackheath mission administrator, said: 'We would have liked this to be a beginning of revival for London, but perhaps that's still to come.'

Chapter 13

SPECIAL MINISTRIES

During both phases of Mission to London Luis Palau shared the Gospel with groups of children, students, women, businessmen, ethnic minorities, entertainers, sports personalities, doctors and members of Parliament. Some of the campaign's greatest success stories emerged from these outreaches to smaller, specialised groups.

CHILDREN, NOAH'S ARK AND THE RAINBOW SPECIAL

An independent follow-up study by MARC found that 24 per cent of the mission's phase two enquirers were less than fourteen years old.

The children's outreach committee was led by Cathy Smith, Scripture Union missions coordinator, who in early 1983 began preparing by researching existing children's ministries and discovered 'not much work was being done in London as a whole regarding children's ministry. No one was giving it a real good kick. Mission to London has given us the kick we needed.'

American missionary Janet Morgan, who helped Smith to coordinate the children's outreach, agreed: 'My eyes have been opened. London needs children's workers desperately. Someone needs to train people not only to teach Sunday school, but also to care for, love and nurture children.'

To this end Smith gathered able volunteers to help plan the children's outreach. Then hundreds of children's counsellors were trained.

The climax of the mission's children's ministry was the Rainbow Special on 23 June 1984 at QPR. For six months, Cathy assisted by Janet and Joan MacLeod, both Mission to London staff members, planned each detail of the programme.

More than eighteen thousand children and parents, some travelling in coach parties from 100 miles away, crowded in. The programme revolved around the story of Noah's Ark. While a dozen actors portrayed Noah's story, others unfurled giant colourful ribbons across the pitch to depict the rainbow of God's promise after the flood.

Dressed casually in jeans and a huge rainbow-coloured bow tie, Palau told the Bible story about Noah, related it to the Gospel, and asked children to receive Christ in their hearts. During a picnic following the programme, children who had made Christian commitments spoke with the hundreds of specially trained children's counsellors in the crowd. The counsellors collected the names of 2,592 children who said they had prayed to receive Christ.

Throughout both phases of the mission, children from all over London wrote letters to ask Palau questions and to pledge their support. One child wrote: 'The meeting was so good that I am going to write out the message and give it to my friends and enemies at school. I don't care how much it will cost. I will still do it.'

Another wrote: 'My dad is dead now. Please I would like to know more of the Luis Palau meetings in Croydon where my brothers, sisters and I were in a children's home. Now we are all separated. I don't know where some of them are living.

'Can you pray for us and our mum, who is not allowed to have our address? I am not allowed to give mine either. I am in a foster home. I am still at school and am the youngest. Can you write and tell me about Jesus, please?'

Another wrote: 'Can you tell me about Mission to London at the QPR football grounds, as my nephews, mother, dad, and I are all football mad, and we don't go to church now at all.'

A nine-year-old wrote: 'The mission is one of the greatest things that has ever happened to me. I came forward the second time I visited the mission. I promise I will pray for the mission every night. I am a very keen member of the choir and am loving every minute of it.'

When Palau spoke to several hundred children at a Saturday morning rally during phase one, 100 children accepted the Lord. A boy named Simon brought two of his unbelieving friends, and both of them received Christ. A boy who heard the Saltmine Band perform an evangelistic concert at his Wimbledon school attended the mission meeting that night, and gave his life to Christ. A young child received Christ the night his own father shared his testimony on the platform at QPR.

Smith summed up the mission's outreach to children: 'The Luis Palau Team coming to this country has given London a push that's made people think more about children and family ministries. We needed that push to stir us into action. Through the mission many children have come to know Jesus, and many others have gone further in their walk with God.'

INSPIRING YOUTH

Mission to London took the Gospel to the city's youth via various evangelistic concerts and rallies in schools and on the streets.

Christian musicians including the Saltmine Band and New Beginnings visited London schools to sing, talk with students about Christ and invite them to the mission meetings.

A Christian teacher in one of the schools visited wrote of these successful concerts: 'What an inspiration to see a team so on fire with the Gospel and with so much humility, openness and insight too. It was the most inspiring day of the whole of my teaching career. Your visit has left a deep impression on the pupils, and they are keen to come to QPR.'

In an all-boys school the Christian Union leader said: 'The boys are tough nuts to crack with religion, but boy, do they need it.' Christians began praying for the boys, and at least five of them received Christ at a mission meeting for youth.

In January 1984 10,000 members of London's Christian

youth groups packed the Royal Albert Hall during two nights as Palau encouraged them to get involved in the mission.

A girl who was a new Christian brought five friends to the mission and three received Christ. She wrote: 'Jesus came into my life only a few months ago, but it's only in the last few weeks, through Mission to London, that I've really gained confidence in talking about Him.'

After a young man received Christ during phase one, he brought a friend to church and his friend also gave his life to Christ. His friend brought another friend, who also became a Christian, who in turn, led his brother-in-law to the Lord. The first young man and his friend booked twenty-five coach seats to bring other unsaved friends to QPR Stadium to hear the Gospel.

London's youth also supported Mission to London financially. One girl who sent £178 to the mission office wrote: 'I am sending you all my money. I felt that God was challenging me to see whether my money or obedience to Him was more important. As you can see I felt my obedience to Him was a billion times more important.'

Not only did young people play a major part in letting London hear the Gospel, but they were also eager to hear the voice of God themselves. Teens aged 14 to 18 made up a third of all inquirers during both phases of the mission. Many of these youths related exciting stories of how Christ had changed their lives during the mission.

A coachload of students from a Sussex girls' school came to QPR, where twenty-five received Christ. Ten girls who didn't attend the meeting decided to give their lives to Christ when they saw the changes in their friends. A young atheist attended the mission's youth night meeting, and after thinking about the Gospel all night, gave his life to Christ the next morning.

A vicar's rebellious daughter had spent some nights away from home, and returned with no explanation. Her father decided he wouldn't let her out of his sight, and took her to the mission with him. During the invitation, the vicar sat with his head bowed – until he saw a familiar pair of feet and legs clad in tennis shoes and leg warmers walk forward. His daughter surrendered her life to Christ that night, and was greatly transformed in the days following.

During Palau's mission in Croydon, twenty-five boys from an area boarding school surrendered their lives to Christ. This was the beginning of a new movement of the Holy Spirit throughout that school.

MINISTRY TO LONDON'S WOMEN

The MARC study found that 24 per cent of all phase two enquirers were women over 18 years old.

London women demonstrated an unusually high responsiveness to the Gospel at thirteen coffee mornings around the city during the mission. Palau addressed 9,300 women at these special meetings, and 1,350 made decisions for Christ.

During phase two Palau spoke at six evangelistic coffee mornings for women accompanied by musician Graham Kendrick and mime artist Geoffrey Stevenson. These well-attended meetings attracted a total of 5,670 women, with 750 responding to the Gospel. At one meeting, 1,050 women arrived to fill 400 available seats, so a nearby overflow venue was arranged. At the Croydon venue, 1,300 women were expected, but 1,700 arrived.

The large attendance and enthusiasm of the women at the coffee mornings so impressed Palau that he said: 'If young people, men and ministers were as excited about the Gospel as the women at these coffee mornings, we would have a revival in Britain.'

One of the more than nine hundred women who packed the Ilford Palais to hear the evangelist, said: 'I thought it was a Harrod's sale when I saw the queues. As soon as we opened the doors of the Palais, women of all ages and sizes rushed in. I've never seen anything like it.'

The women involved in the mission worked diligently to tell London's women that Luis Palau was coming to QPR. They divided London's 366 postal districts among them and each woman informed the women's leaders in the district's churches of forthcoming events and encouraged them to become involved in the mission.

American Roberta Wollen, who for thirty years ministered with her husband in Luis Palau's church in Portland, Oregon, spoke at five women's meetings. Mrs Wollen encouraged women in their relationship with Christ and motivated them to get involved in the mission's Operation Andrew programme by praying for unbelieving friends and inviting them to the mission. The women's prayers were answered when thousands of women gave their lives to Christ during the mission.

The mother of a mission administrator received Christ at a women's coffee morning on Clapham Common.

Although she was a Christian, a woman whose husband had left her did not realise her great worth in Christ. Not until she heard Palau speak to women did she see how much Jesus loved her.

COMMUNICATING TO MEN

Reaching London's adult male population with mass evangelism was more difficult than reaching women, children or youth. The MARC follow-up study reported that only 11 per cent of all phase one enquirers and 10 per cent of phase two enquirers were males over twenty-five years old.

David Pickford spoke of one luncheon attended by more than four hundred businessmen, where thirty-six received Christ.

When Ian Leitch addressed 800 businessmen at a lunchtime service, fifty responded to the Gospel.

A respectable gentleman, a member of the Church of England who regularly attended church, admitted he was not a Christian. When he heard the Gospel during a mission meeting, he recalls: 'I just knew then I had to give myself to Christ.' He *did* give his life to Christ that night in the presence of his Christian wife and sons.

During QPR a London stockbroker with 600 major clients opened his newsletter with these words: 'Luis Palau is an

Argentine evangelist and I want you to hear him.' He then wrote more details of the mission before reporting any information regarding his stockbrokerage.

Palau said: 'This is marvellous. One of the greatest side effects of this campaign is the number of Christians who are getting bold in witnessing for Jesus Christ.'

A businessman who heard Palau speak on the Scripture passage of the rich man getting into heaven said he was 'shaken to the core' by the message. He returned alone another night and gave his heart to Christ. He said: 'I had been a hard and bitter person for a long time, but after I met Jesus Christ I felt the bitterness draining from me. I became a different person.'

MINISTRY TO MINORITIES

More than one million Londoners are from non-Western religious and cultural backgrounds, mostly from the Indian subcontinent. Through Mission to London the Gospel touched the lives of individuals from the Jewish, Muslim, Buddhist, Hindu, Jehovah's Witness and Rastafarian religions. A total of 166 people from these other religious backgrounds publicly responded to the Gospel at QPR.

During phase one Palau's twin sons, Kevin and Keith, arrived in London after completing an intensive, eight-week training course in Muslim evangelism in New York City. In hopes of ministering to some of London's 500,000 Muslims, Kevin and Keith based their evangelism in East London's Henry Martyn Training Centre, an Asian-operated organisation which ministers to Hindus, Sikhs and Muslims. By visiting door to door they befriended several Muslims and shared the Gospel many times.

One Sikh friend called the twins to tell them he had attended the final meeting at QPR, bought some of Palau's books, and told other friends about the mission.

Christians distributed more than six thousand invitations to QPR in Golder's Green, home of many of London's Jewish residents. One man who was praying about how to approach the Jewish residents with the Gospel felt the Lord telling him to invite people to QPR. Enough Jewish Londoners were converted at QPR that a Jewish nurture group was formed.

A young West Indian man who had contact with the Rastafarian and Jehovah's Witness religions attended a mission meeting. Later he sought a mission counsellor and began attending a local church and nurture group.

The sister of a Mission to London secretary had been a Buddhist for nine years. She attended the mission to hear the Gospel, and committed her life to Christ. Now she says she has found the peace she could not find as a Buddhist.

A fifteen-year-old Chinese Christian wrote: 'My family is Buddhist, and so was I until I discovered there is a God who answers prayers. Ever since I invited Jesus into my life, my family think I have gone mad. I love my family. Will you please pray for them? I will be bringing some non-Christian friends to QPR to hear you preach the Gospel.'

A Turkish Christian who manages a sporting goods store brought his Greek assistant to QPR, and the Greek opened his heart to Christ. Together they brought five more employees to QPR and all five received Christ.

During a week's Spanish-language ministry, more than fifty Hispanics made Christian commitments.

Choosing to follow Christ sometimes involves great risk. When a Sikh woman and her daughter became Christians and were baptised, the woman's husband abandoned her and their three children. But the woman and daughter remained faithful to Jesus Christ and brought the other two children to QPR, where both received Christ.

Two men who had been sent from their Arab nation to Britain for job training insisted on seeing Palau at QPR. One fell to his knees, clasped Palau's hand, and began kissing it – a form of respect usually reserved for Muslim holy men. 'I want to become a Christian,' he said. 'You are the one who is supposed to show me how.'

'Two weeks ago I had a dream – a vision from God. In this vision I felt myself drowning, but couldn't do anything to save myself. Then a kind man who appeared before me reached out his hand and saved me. This man was Jesus and

He told me that someone would be provided to tell me how to be saved. I wondered what this dream could mean.

'My friend, who has a Christian background, suggested we attend a local church. There we heard about your meetings and I knew you were the one Jesus was speaking of in my dream. So here I am. What must I do to become a Christian?'

The evangelist reminded the man of the possible persecution – even death – he might face in his country if he decided to follow Christ. The man replied: 'I am willing to die for Christ.'

After Palau explained the Gospel, the Muslim man prayed to receive Christ and a few weeks later was baptised by the evangelist in a London church. As his training in London ended, the man returned to his country, hoping to share the life-changing Gospel with his family, at risk to his life.

Chapter 14

PHASE ONE FINALE – WEMBLEY ARENA

Phase one's climactic conclusion on 21 and 22 October 1983 at Wembley Arena attracted a total of 18,000 people transported via coach from a forty-mile radius.

Special guests seated on the platform at Wembley included a husband and wife who had been converted to Christ at the Palau Team's 1977 campaign in Cardiff. Six years later they were still following Christ and testifying to the lasting effects of mass evangelism.

Also on the platform were delegations of German and Swedish evangelical Christians who had travelled to London to invite Palau to lead crusades in their countries. The evangelist had been enthusiastically received by more than forty thousand at the Ralingsas Conference in Aneby, Sweden, only four months earlier.

The Rev. Ian Coffey hosted the first night at Wembley and the Rev. Lyndon Bowring hosted the final night.

Palau was so thrilled with Scottish soloist Isobel Lindsay's music ministry during his 1981 Glasgow campaign that he asked her to sing at Wembley as well. After she sang 'I Surrender All', he expressed his hopes that many would 'surrender all' that night as they heard the Word of God.

Guest speaker Colonel Jim Irwin, a member of the Apollo 15 crew which gathered the first moon rocks in 1971, told about God's work in his own life. Before flying to the moon, Irwin was a silent Christian who attended church but never shared the Gospel.

Irwin explained: 'I lived for aviation. I thought I could find great satisfaction in flying high and fast, and when I became an astronaut, I thought I would find satisfaction by flying in space. Ultimately, I sought satisfaction in flying to the moon.

'But the Lord works in mysterious ways. Using the Apollo 15 flight to capture my attention, He allowed me to travel far from the earth in order to return with a new love for Him and desire to serve Him. Standing on the moon, I saw the earth as few see it – a little blue marble – a beautiful jewel in the blackness of space.

'Since seeing the earth as God must view it, my life will never be the same. As I looked at the tiny earth, John 3:16 came to mind and I was reminded of His great love for each of us. Flying high and fast will never satisfy. Even reaching the moon doesn't satisfy. Only the love of Jesus Christ can transform lives and truly satisfy.'

Luis Palau addressed the audience: 'When I asked a minister his favourite Mission to London testimony, he told me the exciting story of his daughter's conversion. As a teenager she had rebelled against her parents and refused to attend church. Later she married a godless man, and their two children never stepped inside a church building. One night she visited her parents, who were on their way to an area mission. They were overjoyed when she came with them and surrendered to Christ. When she went home to tell her husband that she had become a Christian and wanted to start attending church, she thought he would be angry. She was thrilled by his response: "You can go to church on one condition. You must take our children with you."'

Palau told another mission testimony of changed lives in Christ: 'A wife who professed to be a Christian had been unfaithful to her husband for four years. She attended family night at an area mission, was convicted of her sins and went forward to give herself completely to Christ. After speaking with a counsellor, she told her extramarital lover that she had rededicated her life to the Lord and that their relationship was finished. When she confessed her sins to her husband she expected he would throw her out of their home. But her weeping husband completely forgave his wife as well as the other man. Today their lives have changed dramatically.

Together they read the Bible and pray, and Jesus Christ is the centre of their home.

'If the Lord can change the lives of those who have been struggling, He can work in your life here tonight.

'You say: "Luis, I was christened as a boy" or "I was confirmed later on". That's good, but have you ever personally opened your heart to Christ? Have you ever asked Jesus Christ to be the God of your life? Does Jesus Christ rule in your heart – yes or no? That's the question.

'All of us must decide. God brought you here tonight. He wants you to make a decision. The Lord is speaking to your heart. The Bible says that Jesus says: "I stand at the door and knock. If anyone hears My voice and opens the door, I will come in to him, and eat with him, and he with Me."

'I opened the door of my life to Christ thirty-five years ago. In all these years I've had my ups and downs, but I've never doubted that I have eternal life, because the Lord Jesus came into my heart and gave me the assurance of eternal life.

'The Bible says that He who began the good work in you will bring it to completion at the day of Jesus Christ. You let Christ come into your heart tonight, and He will begin to work in your life. He will work in you and transform you into the image of Jesus Christ. But you must decide. Open your heart to the living Christ tonight.'

AFTERMATH OF WEMBLEY

When the evangelist invited people to walk forward to publicly commit their lives to Christ, the choir softly sang 'Amazing Grace' while hundreds streamed forward towards a new life in Christ. All barriers were broken that night.

When the enquirers and counsellors had filed into the room behind the platform, the audience continued to sing and to praise God. Even after the musicians had stopped playing and began packing up their instruments, people lingered just a little longer and continued to sing songs to the Lord.

In the *Church of England Newspaper* Anne Townsend wrote of Wembley: 'No one gave the impression of trying to impress anyone. It was this very ordinariness of everything that convinced me of God's touch on that evening. Only God could have taken such ordinary people from so many differing church and denominational backgrounds, and welded them together into a working relationship that could stand the strains of taking a dream of Mission to London and turning it into the reality of the last seven weeks.

'I looked for, but could not find emotionalism that evening; nor emotional blackmail being applied; nor pressure exerted on people to make decisions to follow Christ for motives other than wanting to get right with God . . .

'When Luis gave his simple closing appeal . . . it was so ordinary and devoid of emotional pressure that only God could have brought out the stream of people who came forward . . . Only God could have achieved what has happened in the last seven weeks of Mission to London. When Luis Palau and Lyndon Bowring both ended the evening with the words, "To God be the glory", they were right.'[1]

SENDING THE GOSPEL VIA SATELLITE

To enable more people to benefit from the mission and to pray for its impact, the Wembley meetings were relayed to the United States via satellite for distribution by the Moody Broadcasting Network. The network also transmitted a series of Mission to London documentary reports produced by Nick Page, BBC and freelance Christian broadcaster.

Stan Jeter, senior radio and television producer for the Palau team, supervised the planning and execution of the broadcasts.

'Our experience with Moody's radio network across the United States was a practical example of Christians pooling their resources to take the Gospel far beyond their normal limitations. It also helped lay the foundation for the many similar partnerships we would need for the world-wide broadcasts of Commonwealth 84 the following year,' Jeter said, speaking of the plans to broadcast a portion of Mission to London phase two to more than fifty English-speaking nations world-wide.

Luis Palau said: 'Our goal is to speak to millions about Christ and to raise the visibility and awareness of evangelism. Then we want to work with the churches in these areas — giving them tools with which to evangelise in their own areas of influence.'

To this end, churches in the US cities served by the Moody Network participated by encouraging members and others to listen to the broadcasts. These churches also coordinated the follow-up for those who responded to the crusade message in their local area. The Palau Team prepared special follow-up materials to help these churches to develop their own local evangelistic efforts based on the broadcasts.

In December 1983 a letter in the *Baptist Times* perhaps best summarised the mission's impact on the more than two hundred thousand who attended its first phase: 'My wife and I went to hear Luis Palau speaking the Word of God and it was most refreshing. The Lord really used Luis — Wembley Arena was filled with the Spirit of God. God was moving all around His people, filling them with awe . . . Mission to London was a big success. God's Word found and touched the people, and it was a man who had to travel at least 6,000 miles to tell them. Thank God for this wonderful moment in our lives.'[2]

Chapter 15

NURTURING CHRISTIAN MATURITY

Critics of mass evangelism say new converts are left to fend for themselves once the campaigns have ended. But Mission to London utilised an effective follow-up plan to immediately integrate the mission's enquirers into London's churches.

The Rev. Roy Pointer, church growth consultant for the Bible Society, said mass evangelism has been 'notoriously weak' in caring for new Christians in the past. 'We are determined that this should not be the case in London. Courses for counsellors and Christian nurture ensure that churches know how to care for the enquirers. God is undoubtedly at work through Mission to London. Churches must not miss this opportunity to regain lost ground and reach our capital for Christ.'

Mission to London staff member David Greenaway, a member of the British Church Growth Association Council, said: 'I am greatly encouraged by the Mission to London field team's findings which indicate that 76 per cent of all phase one enquirers are still attending church or nurture groups.'

Greenaway attributed these tremendous statistics to the mission being initiated by and tied into the local church, effectively training Christians in grass-roots evangelism and equipping churches to receive new believers, and encouraging the new Christian's growth and integration into the local church.

This successful follow-up scheme consisted of enquirer counsellors, bridge-builders and nurture groups.

ENQUIRER COUNSELLING

In various places throughout Greater London Christian
leaders taught a three-hour course called Christian Life and
Service Classes, designed to train counsellors to help enquirers who responded to the invitation at the mission. Those
attending were not obliged to counsel at QPR, but those who
wished to could apply to become counsellors and bridge-
builders.

Several people received Christ while taking these classes.
Anglican vicar the Rev. Bob Groves wrote to Palau: 'One of
our church members who has been attending the Christian
Life and Service classes just called to say she has given her life
to Christ. Praise the Lord! He is good.'

About eight thousand trained counsellors served during
the mission. After offering the invitation to receive Christ,
Luis Palau publicly counselled enquirers on how to enjoy a
fulfilling relationship with Christ: read the Bible and pray
daily, tell others about Christ, attend and serve in a church
where Christ is preached and share Christ's love with others.

Each person who came forward at a Mission to London
meeting spoke with a mission counsellor and received Christian literature, but this alone is not enough to ensure that
people continue to grow in their faith. The fellowship of the
local church is vital to their growth, and a scheme called
bridge-builders provided this link.

BRIDGE-BUILDERS

In the bridge-builder scheme, enquirers were set on the road
to mature discipleship, local churches grew in numbers and
bridge-builders acquired skills valuable to the local church.
The job of the bridge-builder was to contact those referred to
them by their local church, care for them by offering help,
encouragement and fellowship at an individual level, attend
the nurture group with the enquirer and introduce them to
the local church.

No time was lost in making the first contact with each

enquirer. Within seventy-two hours of receiving an en-quirer's card, the bridge-builder contacted him and arranged a meeting where the bridge-builder explained the nurture group scheme and encouraged the enquirer to read the Bible and pray daily.

Six weeks after the bridge-builder received the card, he made his last visit to the enquirer to ensure that the person was developing an understanding of the church and was taking an active part in it.

NURTURE GROUPS

Enquirers were channelled into churches with specially-trained nurture groups. Each nurture group consisted of a leader, three or four bridge-builders and three or four new converts. These weekly groups met in homes for at least six weeks for a series of basic Bible studies which introduced the enquirers to Christianity and eased them into the life of the local church.

One nurture group with nine converts added seven more enquirers within three months, and finished with thirty-six people attending the group.

Harvey Thomas said: 'The extent of training and in-depth planning . . . for Mission to London is as great as there has ever been . . . The tremendous depth and concern in the whole training, counselling, and follow-up programmes will move beyond any previously attempted, and I know will be much honoured by the Lord.'[1]

One nurture-group leader said: 'If you follow the material produced for nurture groups by Mission to London, it's a first-rate way of establishing new Christians in the church.'

FAMILY COUNSELLING

At each Palau crusade family counselling centres are set up to provide in-depth biblical counsel for people struggling with deep-seated problems.

The Rev. Jim Williams joined the Luis Palau Evangelistic
Team in 1968. He launched the team's first counselling
centre at Palau's 1972 crusade in Costa Rica. By the mid-
1970s the demand for Williams' counselling was so over-
whelming that Williams started teaching a nine-hour biblical
counselling course to train local Christians to help with the
specialised in-depth counselling at each crusade site. Today
Williams' course has been expanded to twenty hours.

Approximately fifty people who took Williams' course
volunteered to staff the family counselling centre at QPR.
The centre was open Monday through Saturday from 10 a.m.
to 5 p.m. A twenty-seven-year-old volunteer named Brigit
Campbell cleared six weeks from her schedule to organise the
centre, and provided valuable assistance.

Williams said the quality of family counsellors at Mission
to London was 'even better than expected'. He added that
most were well-educated and represented people-oriented
occupations: social workers, nurses, medical doctors and
pastors.

Although counsellors at the centre led nine people to
the Lord during QPR, Williams said: 'The large percentage of people who came to us were Christians struggling
with some aspect of the Christian life, and how to cope
with it.'

Williams said one of the major problems in those coming
to the family counselling centre for help was uncontrolled
sexual desire. Many wondered if God's power could bring
it under control. Williams found that loneliness was a con-
tributing factor in most of these cases. Other recurring
problems included depression, homosexuality and drug and
alcohol abuse.

Family counselling centre volunteer Peter Hider said:
'The counselling centre has given us an army of people who
can return to their own churches and share with others the
training they've received, so that others can be equipped.
The centre wouldn't be necessary if the churches were
fulfilling their function.'

HOME BIBLE STUDIES

Home Bible studies, set up by the local church to evangelise an area, consist of Christians inviting their neighbours into their homes for informal discussions about the Bible.

The Rev. Al Wollen, author of *God at Work in Small Groups*, led several five-hour seminars teaching London's Christians how to lead evangelistic home Bible study groups.

He explained: 'House group evangelism is two-fold. First, it brings together Christians to learn how to interact with each other through dialogue, and assist each other in living the Christian life in a practical way. We need to restore a higher level of visibility and practicality of the daily Christian life. In that kind of atmosphere, the unchurched can see Christianity at work.

'From this comes the second aspect – Christians bringing the unchurched into their midst. Home Bible studies become the bridge between the unchurched and the church service. Evangelism is just beginning to surface in the house group activities. We must be convinced that evangelism isn't something that's done by somebody else. Every Christian is an evangelist. Each of us is responsible to reach an unsaved and unchurched world.'

Later a British church leader told Wollen, 'You are sowing seeds that will change the face of the church in years to come.'

SECTION FOUR

PHASE TWO –
QPR AND BEYOND!

Chapter 16

COUNTDOWN TO QPR

With phase one of Mission to London finished, the mission staff took a quick breath before plunging into the massive task of organising phase two – the central meetings at Queen's Park Rangers' football stadium in June and July 1984. Because this second phase was the major thrust of the two-part campaign, it required enormous planning and preparation.

Mission organisers planned to raise 1·1 million pounds, visit four million homes with personal invitations to the mission, and book 300 coaches for QPR daily. Reaching these mammoth goals in a metropolis as cold to the Gospel as London would have been impossible if God had not been working mightily in the capital.

Palau voiced his hopes for the mission's second phase: 'My dream is that every English-speaking Londoner hears the Gospel. Secondly, that the media will objectively cover the crusade, and even give wings to the Gospel by carrying it across the English-speaking world. Thirdly, I would like to see the stadium filled with at least 50 per cent unbelievers each night, especially on weekends. Fourthly, I would like to see 20,000 confess Christ as a result of the campaign, and see 70 per cent of them incorporated into churches.

'Fifthly, I would like to see Britain enthused about the Gospel, overflowing with a new wave of missionary interest, and her Bible colleges and seminaries jammed with converts entering the ministry. I would like to see ministers who have been cold to evangelism turn their churches around and really honour the Lord.'

On 27 May, dedicated 'Luis Palau Mission to London

Sunday', churches throughout London and the Home Counties prayed for a renewal of spirit before the mammoth QPR meetings began.

Many of these churches echoed in their prayers Palau's hopes for the mission.

London's Christians felt responsible for meeting the mission's costs and urged the executive committee to avoid seat-to-seat offerings during the meetings. They gave generously during the preparation period, through a gift envelope distributed with the nightly programme in the stadium and through thank offerings after the event.

Not all of the finances came from London, or even from within the borders of England. Love gifts came from around the globe, from Scotland to Malta to the United States.

Hundreds of Christians excited for the mission wrote to Palau to encourage him and to assure him of their support. One wrote: 'Thank you for your willingness to be used by God in London by preaching the Gospel message of salvation. Your burden for lost souls is infectious. This morning I found myself asking God to give me a real compassion for lost souls so that I would want to talk to others about Jesus. God save me from being uncompassionate and selfish in keeping Jesus to myself.'

Another wrote: 'I am writing to tell you about my conversion and the wonderful change in my life since I accepted Jesus as my Lord and Saviour at a Mission to London youth meeting. I was brought up as an atheist and was very unhappy at home. But since accepting Christ, my life has changed dramatically. Now my home life is much better and I am actually getting to know my family. Many of my non-Christian friends attended my baptism on Easter Sunday. I pray they will come nearer to God through my witness.

'In this important year may God bless you, Billy Graham, and the Mission to London and Mission England meetings. I pray that many people will come to know Christ and to share a close relationship with our dynamic living Lord.'

Chapter 17

PHASE TWO – QPR!

George Russell, chairman of the Palau team's European Board of Directors, hailed a taxi in London. When the driver asked his destination, Russell said: 'I'm going to QPR stadium to hear Luis Palau.'

The driver replied: 'One of my recent passengers – a successful businessman – just told me that anyone who could put six thousand or more people at QPR or any other place in London for six weeks has something to offer.'

After thinking quietly for a moment, the driver added: 'I intend to go to hear Luis Palau at QPR with my children.'

The QPR dedication service on 30 May 1984 was attended by 7,000 counsellors, stewards, choir members and other mission workers – twice the number mission organisers expected. More than fifty church-chartered coaches delivered thousands to the stadium on opening night.

As Palau knelt with Christian leaders the Rev. Gilbert Kirby prayed for the evangelist and quoted the Scripture: 'Unless the Lord builds the house, its builders labour in vain' (Psalm 127:1).

While Kirby prayed others laid hands on Palau and his team as they were set apart for the work that lay ahead: six weeks of evening meetings and numerous daytime meetings and media interviews.

That night Palau shared this telegram from Billy Graham with the audience: 'All of us pledge our prayers and support for the Mission to London. It is our prayer that God will pour out a blessing that will lead to revival and renewal and that thousands may find Christ as their Saviour.'

During the enthusiastic dedication service hundreds of

Christians stood to recommit their lives to Jesus Christ and to
rededicate themselves to the crusade's theme: Let the whole
of London hear the voice of God. Following the unemotional
invitation people of every age, background and denomination poured on to the pitch to make Christian commitments.

The QPR audience was tremendously enthusiastic, especially the choir. One Christian observing the meetings said:
'The spirit of the meetings is marvellous.' Another said he
noticed 'an incredible stillness and reverence among the
crowd – a tremendous atmosphere of worship'. Another
observed: 'The people are very attentive and responsive.'

Mission to London was not enthusiastically received by all
Londoners. On opening night a few shouting protestors ran
on to the pitch and threw leaflets denouncing religion as a
drug and Luis Palau as a pusher. In another organised effort,
vandals pasted 'cancelled due to revolution' stickers on
Mission to London advertising posters throughout the
city.

Because of opposition by nearby residents the stadium's
sound system could be used only from 8 p.m. to 9:30 p.m.
Thus Palau's messages had to be crisp and brief. The local
residents' understandable fears of traffic noise and crowd
problems were unfounded with the compliant QPR crowds.

THE QPR PROGRAMME

On 5 June Cliff Richard shared the platform with Palau.
More than thirteen thousand attended the meeting and 687
made public commitments to Christ.

On 13 June some fifteen thousand people filled the stands
and spilled on to the pitch to hear Cliff Richard and Sheila
Walsh.

Palau preached on 1 Corinthians 6, and spoke about sex,
temptation and God. Suddenly the audience was no longer
smiling and laughing. Instead they listened intently as the
evangelist explained how they could be free from the chains
of immorality and receive eternal life.

The response was so great that although 1,074 enquirers spoke with crusade counsellors, hundreds more left the stadium before speaking to a counsellor and providing a record of their name and address. More than half of those who did speak with counsellors that night were making first-time decisions for Christ.

After the meeting Palau remarked: 'One of the most encouraging factors of this mission has been the percentage of people making first-time commitments to Christ.'

Attendance for the QPR meetings passed the 150,000 mark on 23 June, the mission's midway point. The average response rate was 6 per cent.

On 27 June 10·2 per cent of the audience made Christian commitments – a Palau team record in Britain.

'These are by far the largest evangelistic meetings to be held in London for close to twenty years,' said Peter Meadows. 'This, and the numbers responding to the message, are a tremendous encouragement.'

Palau said: 'The percentage of the audience receiving Christ was so consistently high that I believe it reveals a hunger for the Word of God. It reveals that Christians will witness to their friends and bring them to hear the Gospel when it's preached in a way acceptable to non-Christians.'

DR GRAHAM AND OTHER GUESTS

Throughout Mission to London special guests sat on the platform to show their support for the mission. These included clergy representing various denominations, British evangelists, Christian leaders, Christian sports personalities and delegations inviting Palau to have crusades in various countries.

By far the most well-known platform guest was American evangelist Billy Graham, who in a 23 June surprise visit to the mission, declared his 'complete support' for Palau and preached a short sermon to the audience of 8,000.

He declared that one of 'the greatest needs' in both Britain and America 'is a renewal and revival in the Church, so that we have a new church, a church that is set on fire by the Holy Spirit.

'Jesus said: "I've come to make you fishers of men,"' said Graham. 'I don't know any better fishing ground in all the world than London.'

On 6 June, the fortieth anniversary of the D-Day Allied landings in Normandy, platform guest Fred Elcock recalled how he had lost his leg in a shell blast as a soldier at Normandy, but his faith in Christ had sustained him. 'May this be D-Day for you, the day you discover Christ,' Elcock exhorted.

Baptist, Anglican, Methodist and Salvation Army clergy were among those who sat on the platform. These included the Rev. John Stott, rector emeritus of All Souls Langham Place; Rev. Arthur Thompson, president of the London Baptist Association; Commissioner Francy Cachelin of the Salvation Army; Dr Donald English, general secretary of the Home Mission Division of the Methodist Church; and Rt Rev. Geoffrey Stuart Snell, Bishop of Croydon.

During the mission, Palau, his team and the mission's staff and executive committee gathered to break bread, to pray for one another and to ask God to pour out His Spirit on London, and especially on her churches.

Several churches from Greater London and the Home Counties hired Operation Andrew coaches to bring non-Christians to QPR. While some churches brought coaches only a few times, others brought coach parties several times each week and some churches filled coaches every night of the crusade.

Local newspapers urged Londoners to take advantage of these church-sponsored coach trips. Thousands did take advantage and many who did found God's free gift of salvation at the stadium. London Transport even arranged special QPR fares on trains, coaches and the underground.

Many Christians hired QPR-bound coaches and filled them with their own non-Christian friends and family.

The city-wide interest in the meetings was so promising that early in the crusade the executive committee decided to extend the mission by two weeks, changing the final meeting from 30 June to 14 July.

Palau said: 'The Gospel is becoming a current topic in this city. We must go on in our effort to let all of London hear the voice of God.'

David Pickford explained: 'We are seeing a steady build-up of interest and support, and the extra twelve meetings will give more opportunity to reach our goal of letting "the whole of London hear the voice of God".'

MASSIVE MEDIA ATTENTION

Palau sometimes had several media interviews per day in addition to preaching at QPR stadium. In addition to his normally very hectic crusade schedule, during one twelve-day period he held a press conference at the Strand Palace Hotel, was interviewed by the *Sunday People*, the *Daily Mirror*, the *Guardian*, the *Church of England Newspaper*, BBC Radio's *World at One*, Independent Radio News, *TV-AM*, *Breakfast TV*, ITV's *Thought for Sunday*, BBC Radio 4 *Today Programme*, the LBC *Brian Hayes Talk Show*, London Weekend Television's *Credo*, Capitol Radio, BBC Radio 2 *Good Morning Sunday*, and *Radio County Sound*. The BBC also recorded a *Songs of Praise* programme at QPR in late June.

Palau said: 'As this media coverage turns the attention of this city to the crusade and the Gospel message, our goal remains the same: Let all of London hear the voice of God.'

A media room including telephones, typewriters, photo-copying machines and a telex was available to accredited journalists at QPR.

Informal surveys found that almost everyone in London had seen the Mission to London posters and was aware of the meetings at QPR stadium. Although some Londoners disliked the advertisements, a surprisingly large number of people came to QPR as a direct response to the publicity and without a personal invitation.

A Portsmouth nurse visiting London was amazed at the number of posters advertising the meetings at QPR stadium. She was curious about the meetings, but had to return to Portsmouth to work that night. The next morning on her way home from work, she saw a poster advertising a special Luis Palau meeting in Portsmouth that very morning. Instead of going home to sleep, she attended the meeting and gave her life to Christ.

The Lord also had His hand on the mission's finances.

After QPR, Mission to London faced a deficit of £155,000 – mostly as a result of the two-week extension.

In early August, two weeks after the mission's conclusion, George Russell said: 'We are confident that God will fully meet our needs. The finance executive has no doubts that the Christians of London will help us, having helped us so far, to reach our target.'

Russell added that the remaining £155,000 left to raise after the mission 'is not a formidable task when you think of the blessing that has come to many churches'.[1]

The finance committee prayed that they would pay all the mission's debts by the end of September. On 29 September the budget had been met and all Mission to London bills had been paid.

The Rev. Gilbert Kirby said: 'This has been possible as a result of generous and sacrificial giving from individuals and churches. To have this level of giving after the event indicates the extent to which people have seen God at work.'

CHANGED LIVES IN CHRIST

Thousands witnessed God at work through the Mission to London meetings, where countless lives were transformed by Christ's love.

An alcoholic was so drunk that people thought he was dead, and rushed him to the hospital. A few days later he went to QPR and received Christ as his Saviour. He told Palau: 'Now I am completely freed from alcohol, and I sing in the QPR choir every night.'

A counsellor who had received Christ at Palau's 1977 crusade in Cardiff wrote to Palau: 'Not all people who come to QPR will feel desperate, lonely and sick. But all will feel emptiness if they don't have Christ and are separated from God, as I was seven years ago.'

The day after a boy received Christ at QPR, he returned some cheese he had stolen from a local shopkeeper a few days earlier. He told the surprised shopkeeper: 'I went to QPR and received Christ. I confess that I stole this cheese, but I want to return it to you. Please forgive me.' The shopkeeper was so touched by the boy's changed heart that he went to QPR to hear the life-changing Gospel himself.

A girl who received Christ during Palau's phase one mission brought her mother to QPR stadium, and led her to Christ.

A man who nearly died from a drug overdose later saw a television programme criticising Palau's lack of social relevancy, and went to QPR. Mentioning the programme, Palau added that the Gospel *is* socially relevant. At the invitation, the man began life again as a new creation in Christ.

A fifteen year-old boy ran away from home after arguing with his older brother. He planned to head for the south coast, but found himself heading for London instead. In London he followed the signs to QPR and entered the stadium. There he saw one of his school mates, who was a Christian. That night he heard the Gospel and gave his life to Christ. Later he said: 'I feel I had to come to London. I don't believe it was a coincidence. I feel so different now.'

A counsellor had no one to counsel at QPR, so he went home. Beside the road he saw a man whose car had stalled, and he stopped to see if he could help. The motorist, who had just been to QPR, had wanted to go forward at the meeting, but didn't have the courage to do so. After fixing the car, the counsellor led the motorist to the Lord as they knelt beside the road.

On 14 July 1984 the year-long Mission to London ended. More than twenty-three thousand people packed the stadium for the closing meeting of the crusade. After the forty nights

of preaching in the stadium home of the Queen's Park
Rangers' football team, a total of 280,000 Londoners had
attended the QPR meetings, and some 19,000 had made
public commitments to Christ at QPR. Another 1,000 made
commitments at smaller daytime mission meetings.

Palau said: 'We've made an impact on London. Although
it's been an exciting, fruitful crusade, and tens of thousands
have heard the Gospel, we still must reach thousands more.'

But for more than a quarter of a million people, QPR
would never again mean football. And for some 19,000 it
would always mean the beginning of a new life with Jesus
Christ.

Chapter 18

COMMONWEALTH 84 –
Sending God's Word to the World

It's 10 p.m. in QPR stadium in West London. Tonight's Mission to London meeting has concluded and the crowds have dispersed, leaving the stadium dark and deserted.

But in the sound studio beneath QPR, radio technicians and engineers reach the height of their evening's work: editing a recording of the night's meeting into a compact, hour-long programme. By midnight their work will be completed and the radio signals of tonight's edited programme will be beamed by cable and satellite to broadcasters around the globe.

By tomorrow night millions of English-speaking people world-wide will have heard tonight's message at QPR via an electronic outreach called Commonwealth 84.

Virtually the entire English-speaking world was linked to Mission to London during Commonwealth 84, which one broadcasting executive termed as 'perhaps the single most important Christian effort in the world' in 1984. Letters from around the globe testify to the far-reaching impact of these broadcasts.

From England: 'I listened to Luis Palau this morning on Trans World Radio. I think it is just the thing we need and I pray that England will break out into a great revival.'

From South Africa: 'The broadcasts helped me to realise that the Gospel message is for all countries all over the world, and the message is the same no matter where it is given, as long as they preach Christ's message of salvation.'

From Zambia: 'I found Palau's message so interesting that

I didn't miss any of his broadcasts. I have decided to accept
Jesus Christ as my Lord and Saviour. Before hearing the
messages I lived away from God.'

From the United States: 'I was in the process of making a
decision of accepting Jesus as my Saviour when I heard the
Commonwealth 84 broadcasts, which pushed me along the
path towards salvation.'

From Kenya: 'I listened to Palau's broadcasts and was very
much blessed. These messages have made me a changed
person, and have restored my relationship with God.'

From Ethiopia: 'Luis Palau's messages were very interesting and encouraging, especially in a country like this where
we have no such religious broadcasts. They helped me to
understand my personal relationship with Jesus Christ.'

From South Africa: 'I benefitted very much from these
messages because I gave my heart to Jesus Christ. I experienced a peace in my heart and now can meet each day
victoriously.'

From the Netherlands Antilles: 'Listening to the sermons
gave me a feeling of joy and peace I had never had before.
Some things I wondered about but didn't have the courage to
ask were answered by Luis Palau. Thank God for that.'

From Kenya: 'Evangelist Luis Palau's messages have built
me up spiritually. They have also challenged many unbelievers to seek the truth about Jesus Christ.'

These letters – and hundreds more like them – record the
success of Commonwealth 84. During the week of 25–30
June 1984 five Mission to London meetings were transmitted
via satellite for same-day or next-day radio broadcasts in
some fifty nations on five continents.

INVALUABLE PARTNERSHIP

Combined with special Mission to London television programmes and a literature campaign, Commonwealth 84 had a
potential audience of 175 million people, many in Third-
World countries. Except for five commercial radio stations in

Canada, all stations donated their time in a united effort to
'let all the English-speaking world hear the voice of God'.

In this invaluable partnership Christian broadcast
agencies, churches and other groups donated their finances,
facilities and expertise to carry the Gospel from London
across the earth. About £66,000 worth of air time was
donated by broadcast organisations which blanketed the
world with short-wave radio coverage of Mission to London.

'The excitement of multiplying the Christian message to
millions, of bringing Christian communities and organisations together for a single event, is both exhilarating and
rewarding,' said Stan Jeter, senior radio and television producer for the Palau team.

'We've been greatly encouraged by the unity we've established with people – most of them volunteers – across some
fifty countries. We have now established a network within
which further growth will undoubtedly follow.'

Participants in Commonwealth 84 included Bible Literature International, ELWA Radio, Far East Broadcasting
Association, Far East Broadcasting Company, HCJB in
Ecuador, Trans World Radio, Moody Broadcasting Network, Northwestern College Radio Network, Trinity Broadcasting Network, and WTKK-TV in Washington DC.

Interdev, an American communications consulting firm,
helped to plan Commonwealth 84 and coordinated the tech-
nical details.

'On a geographical scale Commonwealth 84 represents a
first in the history of Christian broadcasting,' said William
Thatcher, associate director of Interdev.

Jeter said: 'There is just no way the Luis Palau team could
fund and implement this remarkable coverage without the
understanding and willing cooperation of individual Christians and Christian organisations from many countries.'

A number of satellites beamed the Commonwealth broadcasts to the world. Transmitters sent the radio programmes
to continental Europe, Africa, India, Pakistan, Australia,
New Zealand, the Philippines, the Caribbean, Canada and
the United States. British Telecom made the satellite linkups
possible.

Richard Colenso, the Palau Team's North American director, supervised the entire project.

Edward E. Plowman, former news editor of *Christianity Today* magazine, directed the volunteer Commonwealth 84 news team, comprised of journalists from Australia, Canada, Jamaica and the United States.

Les Raker, president of Christian television station WTKK in the Washington, D.C. area, brought a team of six technicians and four tons of video equipment to London to record television segments for North America. Trinity Broadcasting Network (TBN) of California provided a director and cameraman. Forrest Boyd of International Media Service in Washington, DC, Seph Barnard from South Africa and Ray Hosking from Australia also produced Mission to London TV broadcast segments. Subsequently both WTKK and TBN edited and aired numerous London crusade specials with the material they shared.

Television material was made available to participating countries and offered to others world-wide. Mission to London television coverage was aired in Australia, Canada and the United States.

'God watched over the mechanics of this work,' said Phill Butler, director of Interdev. Butler explained that only a few major hitches happened, such as losing contact with a satellite for ten minutes.

'It's a credit to Luis and the team that they were willing to stick their necks out five million miles and trust God,' Butler added.

A project as massive as Commonwealth 84 was not new to the Palau team, which has used satellite-distributed crusade evangelism since the 1970s. In 1975 a similar Palau team plan, Continente 75, extended the Gospel throughout Latin America from Palau's Nicaragua crusade.

Although Continente 75 provided three weeks of crusade broadcasts compared to Commonwealth's six days, the latter extended the Gospel to a much larger audience and geographical area, reaching cultures new to the Palau team's ministry.

Yet another Spanish network, Continente 85, occurred

during Easter Holy Week, 1–7 April, 1985 to extend the Gospel to the entire Spanish-speaking world.

Commonwealth 84 was directly tied to the local church. In countries airing the broadcasts, churches and parachurch organisations persuaded millions to listen and provided counsel to those who made commitments to Christ as a result of the programmes. In Jamaica several churches in rural areas set up radio receivers and had special crusade services the week of the broadcasts, with their special evangelist, Luis Palau, preaching via radio.

With the local churches, the mass media and the Palau team working together, God blessed Commonwealth 84 with life-changing impact upon millions.

Perhaps the success of Commonwealth 84 is best summarised in this letter from a government leader in Grenada: 'Congratulations on superlative Christian radio at its finest. The world needs more of this. You have created a demand for more. What now?'

Chapter 19

RESULTS—
Transformed Lives and Growing Churches

Critics of mass evangelism charge that a crusade's lasting impact – if any – is minimal. But Luis Palau and his team have witnessed incredible lasting results by working closely with local churches to ensure that new converts are followed up and nurtured to Christian maturity.

Many British Christians were still following Christ after making Christian commitments years earlier at evangelistic meetings much like Mission to London.

One woman wrote: 'I was converted through Billy Graham's Harringay crusade thirty years ago. Since then I have served the Lord in my parish church in London. My husband and I have been very involved in bringing people to QPR to hear the life-changing Gospel.'

Another witness to the lasting effects of mass evangelism was a young man who had become a Christian at Palau's 1981 Glasgow crusade. Since then he had attended a youth fellowship, taught Sunday school, served as his university's Christian Union representative and counselled at Billy Graham's Mission England.

On his application for summer evangelism work with London City Mission he wrote: 'Because of this responsibility I have matured in the faith quite considerably, and have felt real joy as God has worked in my life. I hope to eventually become a minister.'

A young man who had been converted through Cliff Richard's ministry three years before QPR served as a coun-

sellor and steward during the mission. He wrote: 'Since
Mission to London I feel God is calling me into full-time
ministry with a Christian organisation.'

The Rev. Michael Cole said: 'I don't see mass evangelism
as contrary to the work of the local church. They both must
go together.'

The Palau team's most phenomenal church growth statistics resulted from Palau's 1976 crusade in Rosario,
Argentina. The church growth principles applied to the
Rosario crusade have since been labelled the Rosario Plan
and are known by church growth experts world-wide.

After the crusade the five-year growth rate for Rosario
churches nearly doubled – from 49 per cent before the
crusade to a projected 92 per cent.[1]

Today magazine reported in its August 1983 issue: 'Shock
statistics claiming that as few as 6 per cent of those going
forward at an evangelistic crusade are still to be found in
churches six months later have given the [mass evangelism]
method a bad press. It is proving difficult to persuade
some church leaders that Mission to London will be any
different.'

The article added that 57 to 67 per cent of all enquirers
from Palau's Rosario crusade and Billy Graham's 1979
Sydney, Australia crusade continued following the Lord.

The article concluded: 'These crusades did lead to long-
term church growth and new churches were successfully
planted.'[2]

After Mission to London ended the *Church of England
Newspaper* reported: 'England has never had such a summer
for hearing the Gospel,' and added that the combined attendance for Mission to London, Mission England and Leighton
Ford's Mission Solent totalled nearly 1·25 million.

'But now the "mass" evangelists have packed their bags
and flown out . . . So where have the efforts of Billy Graham,
Luis Palau and Leighton Ford left us? With a crisis on our
hands.'

The article concluded that Britain's more than 100,000
new converts 'must now depend on their local churches . . .
All this is an enormous challenge to the churches throughout

the country. But we know that many churches themselves are not the same as they were before the missions began.'[3]

EXPLODING CHURCHES

A MARC Europe analysis found that London's churches grew by 1·8 per cent through Mission to London. The analysis revealed that the number of people responding at the mission from Greater London and the Home Counties is equivalent to the number required to start eighty-three new congregations.

Peter Brierley, director of MARC Europe, said, 'If anyone should ask whether it was all worth it, then figures like these indicate a strong answer in the affirmative.'

The Rev. Les Ball witnessed tremendous growth in his church, Clapham Park Baptist – Bonneville, through their involvement in Mission to London. Since the area mission in Clapham, his church added an extra morning service and began planning a larger building to accommodate their incredible growth.

Ball said: 'This is a marvellous witness, as we live in the inner city, where churches are not supposed to grow. We praise God for Mission to London! This has been the highlight of my ministry in south London, where for nine years I have been working and praying for a campaign like Mission to London. It has thrilled my heart to see scores of people mobilised in evangelism, and thousands receive Christ.'

The Rev. Bob Groves, Anglican vicar of All Saints Church in Brixton, said: 'As a result of our involvement in Mission to London, our fellowship has grown by more than 100 per cent. We also have many more truly dedicated Christians and more trained people in the church now. How exciting things are here! The Lord is really working in London, and though there have been difficult times and disappointments, the many blessings and encouragements far outweigh them.

'We have seen spiritual growth in the lives of individuals and numerical growth in home Bible studies and Sunday congregations. Members continue to witness and non-believers continue to be challenged.'

During both phases of the mission, Groves met with other ministers in the Brixton area three times weekly to pray for revival in London and for Mission to London and Luis Palau's part in that revival.

Groves added: 'It has been encouraging, challenging, and rewarding to be part of Mission to London. I will never be the same as I was before the mission.'

Through Mission to London, churches joined in prayer, reached out to their city together and experienced tremendous growth. But these were not the only effects of Mission to London. Another positive result was the large number of London Christians trained to spread the Gospel and to nurture new Christians.

Doug Barnett said: 'One of the Greatest results of Mission to London is the number of Christians who were trained, encouraged and had their faith stirred because they led somebody to the Lord. That will impact the churches in Britain because trained Christians whose faith has been raised by seeing response to the Gospel will not lose that excitement, but will continue sharing the Gospel and expecting things to happen.'

Metropolitan Superintendent to the Baptist Union Arthur Thompson oversees more than two hundred and sixty Baptist churches in London. He said: 'Many churches have told me of plans for their own evangelistic campaigns next year because they want to use those trained as counsellors and nurture-group leaders by Mission to London. Now we have resources available as a result of the stimulus from Mission to London.'

Wesley Richards of Slough Christian Centre wrote: 'We have much to be grateful for through Mission to London. In our three nurture groups we are following up more than thirty new converts, with more in the pipeline. Our congregation's morale has increased at seeing God working through them. We are also realising that the church must be geared to winning people to Christ and trained to nurture new converts.'

An Anglican vicar said his congregation is more interested in evangelism now: 'Even if individuals feel they cannot do much themselves, they do what they can. One very timid pensioner has introduced an avowed atheist to church services. That "atheist" is now asking questions, and believes that God exists.'

Eric Delve said that the missions of Luis Palau and Billy Graham 'touched a deep longing within the ordinary British people for something to give a sense of meaning to their lives in an increasingly mechanised and impersonal technological society.' The missions also revealed the longing of lay Christians for 'leadership which would decisively carry them into events which would bring the church and its message, and above all its Lord, to the attention of the nation'. The church must incorporate 'events . . . which will proclaim our Good News to the people of this country' and 'training in individual witness and group nurture' for the existing Christians.[4]

In another article Delve wrote that in order for new believers to mature 'they must become genuine parts of the body of Christ . . . Our churches must become places where we live, play and work together.'[5]

Many British Christian leaders were disappointed that more London churches did not fully support Mission to London.

George Hider of the London City Mission said: 'The mission provided for Christians and churches an unparalleled opportunity for evangelism which I am sad to say was missed by many . . . I rejoice greatly at the blessing received and yet my lasting impression will be that it was an opening from God that was not entered into by many. I can only implore our capital's Christians to wake up to God-given opportunities . . . May God forgive us and give us yet further possibilities to work at bringing others to Him.'[6]

An Anglican vicar said: 'Having Mission to London and Billy Graham's Mission England in this country at the same time surprised and delighted me as a special answer to prayer. God is reaching for an end beyond human comprehension. I

am convinced that God is gathering His forces to achieve a
mighty end in Britain and the world.'

FAR-REACHING EFFECTS OF MISSION
TO LONDON

The effects of the mammoth Mission to London did indeed
spread far beyond London. Thousands of people around the
world heard the Gospel and committed their lives to Christ.

In October 1984 – three months after Mission to London –
Luis Palau made a guest appearance at Billy Graham's
crusade in Vancouver. After the meeting a young woman
who was serving as a crusade counsellor told Palau her
amazing story.

In 1983 she went to Europe to work as a nanny. In London
she made friends with a Christian girl who took her to hear
Palau speak at Wimbledon Theatre during Mission to
London phase one. She was interested in the Gospel Palau
preached. She also became friends with an American girl
named Linda, a musician with Wings of Light, a group
which performed during the mission. Linda took her to a
women's coffee morning to again hear Palau preach the
Gospel. Here she made her decision.

The young woman told Palau: 'I wanted to give my life to
Jesus Christ because I couldn't get my life together on my
own. When the invitation was given, the Holy Spirit lifted me
off my seat and floated me to the front, where I gave my life to
Christ.'

Shortly afterwards she began a job in Germany as a nanny.
But after beginning her new job, she called her parents,
realised how homesick she was, and decided to return to
Vancouver. 'God put Christians in my path whenever I was in
trouble and needed help in London and Germany. I came
home with the Lord on my side. He calmed my terrible
temper, made me realise my serious sin problems and made
me so very aware of His presence. I came home a changed
person.'

Her friend Linda directed her to a growing Bible-teaching church only five minutes from her home in Vancouver. She began attending the church, joined a Bible study group and later was baptised and began teaching children's Sunday school.

As a counsellor during Billy Graham's Vancouver crusade in October 1984 – exactly a year after giving her life to Christ – she led six people to the Lord. She told Palau: 'Christ daily reveals more of Himself to me, and more about me. I used to be totally insensitive to the needs of others and lived only for me. I now care deeply for those around me, and trust 100 per cent in the Lord and His plans for my future. Now the Lord is gently guiding me to be the woman He wants me to be.'

This young woman who had cared only for herself began studying to be a nurse, and works with the elderly as a nurse's aide at a hospital on weekends. 'I enjoy this job immensely. Eventually I would like to work as a nurse overseas. The Lord works miracles even in this day and age. I'm really growing in His love, and I want to spread His love whenever He provides the opportunity.'

She concluded with this Scripture verse which summarises the tremendous impact of Mission to London on thousands of lives worldwide: 'If anyone is in Christ, he is a new creation; the old has gone, the new has come!' (2 Corinthians 5:17).

A month following the conclusion of Mission to London, Ian Coffey said: 'This is quite a year for evangelism. Arguably, in Britain, there has never been a year like it. Where do we go from here? Nothing is over. We have hardly begun.'[7]

Chapter 20

JESUS CHRIST IS FOR TODAY
by Luis Palau

When Luis Palau preached this sermon to several thousand at London's QPR stadium, more than fifty English-speaking nations heard the Gospel message in the satellite broadcast strategy called Commonwealth 84.

Not long ago when students at the University of Leeds asked me if Christianity is still relevant, I told them: 'I don't know if "Christianity" as you understand it is relevant, but I know that Jesus Christ is very relevant.'

Earlier today I attended the Wimbledon tennis championships and I thought that life, like tennis, never ends in a tie. You either win or lose. Each of us will be either a winner or a loser in life, depending on what we do with Jesus Christ.

I want to read a Bible passage so relevant that it could be in tomorrow morning's newspaper. As I read it, remember that the Bible is the Word of God, inspired by the Holy Spirit. The Bible is without error. You can trust it 100 per cent. Everything it affirms is the truth of God. Although it was written 2,000 years ago, it is relevant tonight here in London and all over the world. Listen to the Word of God.

'Mark this. There will be terrible times in the last days. People will be lovers of themselves, lovers of money, boastful, proud, abusive, disobedient to their parents, ungrateful, unholy, without love, unforgiving, slanderous, without self-control, brutal, not lovers of the good, treacherous, rash, conceited, lovers of pleasure rather than lovers of God – having a form of godliness but denying its power. Have nothing to do with them.

'They are the kind who worm their way into homes and gain control over weak-willed women, who are loaded down with sins and are swayed by all kinds of evil desires . . .

'In fact, everyone who wants to live a godly life in Christ Jesus will be persecuted, while evil men and impostors will go from bad to worse, deceiving and being deceived. But as for you, continue in what you have learned and have become convinced of, because you know those from whom you learned it, and how from infancy you have known the holy Scriptures, which are able to make you wise for salvation through faith in Christ Jesus. All Scripture is God-breathed and is useful for teaching, rebuking, correcting and training in righteousness, so that the man of God may be totally equipped for every good work.

'In the presence of God and of Christ Jesus, who will judge the living and the dead, and in view of his appearing and his kingdom, I give you this charge: Preach the Word; be prepared in season and out of season; correct, rebuke and encourage – with patience and careful instruction. For the time will come when men will not put up with sound doctrine. Instead, to suit their own desires, they will gather around them a great number of teachers to say what their itching ears want to hear' (2 Timothy 3:1–6, 3:12–4:3).

Doesn't this describe the day that you and I are living in? I want to tell you that you can have hope because Jesus Christ is alive.

The Bible says that you can escape the world's corruption by knowing Jesus Christ as your Saviour.

If you reject Jesus Christ, what are your options? The only other option is to live alone and die alone. But if you have Jesus Christ, you have the Word of God, the Spirit of God in your life to give you the assurance of eternal life when you die.

The Bible teaches that Jesus Christ is alive because He rose from the dead. On the cross Jesus died for our sins, but He rose on the third day. Death couldn't hold Him because He's God, the Son of God. That's why Jesus Christ is relevant to you tonight.

You may be a university professor, or a student, single or

married, widowed or divorced, with or without children. But whatever your status, Jesus Christ is relevant to you because He wants to be a part of your life. He is relevant in six areas of our lives.

1. JESUS CHRIST IS ALIVE AND RELEVANT FOR THE SOCIAL ORDER OF OUR NATIONS

Henry Kissinger, former secretary of state in America, once said that less than twenty-five free nations remain in the world today. The truly free nations are those which, like Britain, have had spiritual revivals in the last 200 to 400 years – revivals based on the Bible, the Word of God. Virtually the only nations where citizens don't fear secret police or some kind of dictator are those where Jesus Christ has brought a mighty revival.

Britain's past Christian revivals – in the days of John and Charles Wesley, John Wycliffe, Charles Spurgeon, F. B. Meyer and other great preachers – brought a great awakening to Britain. You enjoy many great blessings here in England because of the influence of past Christian revivals. Under the law you enjoy justice, freedom of worship and freedom of the press. This comes from Christ's impact on your society.

Today's young people don't know this because they have never experienced a spiritual revival. Today millions of young people never attend church. Many young people don't even get married any more.

The Bible teaches us that if we follow the ways of the Lord, He will bless this land. He will bless any land if the people and its leaders will follow His Word. Let's keep praying that through Mission to London and Mission England a wave of revival will sweep the nation. Let's have a tidal wave of revival, thousands of conversions, repentance of sin, faith in the Lord Jesus Christ and salvation all over the land.

Some of you fathers and mothers and grandparents have been away from the Lord for a long time. Some of you have never been converted, and you know it in your heart. Others were converted when you were young, maybe in Crusaders, Boys Brigade, your local church or a Billy Graham campaign. But you walked away and cooled off and haven't been the person you should have been.

You must return to the Lord and you know it.

2. JESUS CHRIST IS ALIVE AND RELEVANT TODAY FOR THE INTELLECTUAL QUEST

People are lonely today. They want to run away and escape, but they don't know how to do it. Some escape with drink, some with drugs. some run from man to man or woman to woman, searching, searching.

Recently a young woman whose job relocated her from a little village to London wrote to us: 'I feel so lonesome and lost.' A man she met was nice to her and showed her the city. She wrote: 'To pay him back, I went to bed with him.' But she added, 'I feel so lonely.'

When she heard the Gospel at QPR Stadium, she realised the satisfaction she was looking for couldn't be fulfilled by a man. But Jesus could fulfil her. She gave her heart to Christ and now she is alive and fulfilled by Jesus Christ.

All of us ask the deeper questions of life: Who am I? Where did I come from? Where am I going? What is the purpose for my being alive? Why did God make me? Whether consciously or unconsciously, this is part of our intellectual quest in life.

The Bible teaches that you are a trinity of body, soul and spirit, and that you are created in the image and likeness of God. You are not an animal, as the secular humanists and atheists would like you to believe. When you die it's *not* all over. The Bible teaches that when you die, you'll be more alive than ever. The only difference will be that until the resurrection you'll be away from your body.

You are a living soul, not an animal. You are not a cow or a horse. You are a man or a woman. You were created in the image and likeness of God. Then why do we feel lonely, lost and empty? Why do we feel unfulfilled?

We are unfulfilled because of the third part of our personality – the spirit. The Bible teaches that all of us are born with our spirit dead – disconnected from God because we belong to the fallen human race. Although we are created in the image of God, we are separated from God because of sin.

When the Bible says that our mothers conceived us in sin, it doesn't mean that our mothers committed sin when they had us. It means that we are born with a sin nature, which we got from our parents and they from their parents, all the way back to Adam and Eve. That is why our spirits are dead. But when you come to Jesus Christ, it's exciting. Suddenly you're alive to God. Jesus Christ is very relevant to the intellectual quest.

A young man's old Ford motor car broke down as he was driving on a motorway in America. The young man tried to repair his car, but couldn't get it started. After some time an enormous limousine stopped beside the old Ford. An old, well-dressed gentleman got out and asked: 'Can I help repair your car?'

The young fellow looked at the old man, his expensive car and clothes and thought: 'What does this rich man know about repairing cars?' He told the man he could do it himself, but after turning this and that it still wouldn't start. Finally the old gentleman said: 'Let me help you. Maybe I can repair it.'

The young man wondered how the old man could possibly repair his broken down car. But a few minutes later the old gentleman told the young man to crank the motor, and the old Ford started. When the young man asked the gentleman how he had known how to repair the car, the gentleman replied: 'I'm Henry Ford. I invented this car.'

Because Ford had invented the car, he knew exactly what was wrong with it. God invented you and knows exactly what's wrong with you too. Tonight He is telling you: 'Give me your heart. I know what's wrong with your heart. I know what's happening in your life.' He is saying to you: 'Young man, young woman, let me come into your life.' He is saying:

'Let me be the master of your family and the king of your home. I invented the man, the woman and the family. I made you the way you are. Let me be your heavenly mechanic. Let me put you together again.'

The Bible says: 'If anyone is in Christ he is a new creation; the old has gone, the new has come!' (2 Corinthians 5:17). If you give your life to Jesus Christ, old things will pass away and all things will become new.

But you must make the decision. You must intelligently come to Christ. God knows you and you can know God. Maybe you know very little about God, but He wants to reveal Himself to you. And when you come to Christ, you will find many of your questions answered in the Bible.

When I was nineteen years old and just beginning my ministry in Argentina, a doctor told me: 'Young man, you almost convinced me to follow Christ, but I don't understand it all. I am a scientist, and I want to understand everything before I give my life to Christ.'

I replied: 'Doctor, first you must take a step of faith and open your heart to Christ. Then you will enter God's family, He will give you His Holy Spirit, and you will begin to understand the Bible.'

We had tea and talked for hours. Finally at about two in the morning this doctor gave his life to Jesus Christ. Today, twenty years later, he is still preaching every weekend, and has led hundreds to Christ. But it all started as a step of faith.

Your intellectual quest will be satisfied deeply when you give your life to Jesus Christ, but you must come by faith. The first step is to bow your knee to your God and ask Jesus Christ into your life.

3. JESUS CHRIST IS ALIVE AND RELEVANT TODAY FOR PSYCHOLOGICAL WORRIES

Today the whole world is afraid. Here in the West we have a feeling of gloom. We fear diseases, missiles, invasion and atomic warfare. But the relentlessness of history is coming to a head. The Bible says that during a war called Armageddon all hell will break loose on earth. The Bible says that one third of the human race will be killed in one hour, one third of the rivers will dry up and one third of the animals and vegetation will be killed. Many believe the Bible is describing an atomic war.

What can we do? We can work for peace and encourage our leaders to work for peace, but in reality we must be ready for that day of Armageddon. You can prepare by having Jesus Christ in your heart. The Bible says: 'The peace of God, which transcends all understanding, will guard your hearts and your minds in Christ Jesus' (Philippians 4:7).

Christians today live in all kinds of societies. Many of them live in oppressive conditions. But all Christians, even those who have been imprisoned, can have peace in their hearts because the Bible promises that God's perfect peace will keep the Christian's heart and mind in Christ Jesus. When you have peace with Christ you have peace with God, peace with your soul and peace with other people.

4. JESUS CHRIST IS ALIVE AND RELEVANT TODAY FOR FAMILY NEEDS

How families are in need of Jesus Christ today! Throughout Britain, North America and Latin America – all over the world – families are hurting and falling apart. Maybe Jesus has had no part in your home, but He should be the centre of our homes. The Bible says we men are to love our wives as Christ loved the church. The Bible says that a wife is to respect her husband and that children are to obey their parents. We parents are to raise our children in the fear of the Lord. God wants to come into your home. He wants to come into your family. Jesus Christ is essential in our homes.

If Jesus Christ wasn't the centre of our home my wife Pat and I would have broken up long ago. I don't know what would have happened to our four boys. But because of Jesus we love and support each other, and my boys are walking with the Lord. Two of them want to be missionaries to win Muslims to the Lord Jesus. We owe it all to Jesus. We're no good in ourselves.

Jesus Christ is alive. He wants to be a part of your family, but you must let him in. The Bible says: 'Believe in the Lord Jesus, and you will be saved – you and your household' (Acts 16:31).

The Lord wants to come into your home through you. Maybe your home is not a Christian home. You want to know the Son of God, but your parents don't want anything to do with Him. Then you come to Christ. And as you open your heart to Christ, you'll go home with Jesus in your heart. And the Lord will begin to change your family through you. The Lord must begin somewhere. Let Him begin with you and your heart.

Perhaps some of you women here couldn't persuade your husbands to come to this stadium. You don't have Christ in your own heart, but you want your husband to come to Christ first. Woman, you come to Christ first and take Him home with you. He will fulfil you, working in you to reach your husband and children. God will use you as a woman.

Some of you men know you need Christ in your home. Come as a man, and say: 'Oh God, I really need You in my home. Lord Jesus, come into my heart.'

5. JESUS CHRIST IS ALIVE AND RELEVANT FOR TODAY IN SEXUAL SATISFACTION AND FREEDOM

The Bible is the manual of the One who made us and who knows all about us. God created sexuality. Sex is one of the most powerful, beautiful forces in the world, yet it can make or break your life.

The Lord made the rule book, and if you play by His rules, you'll be successful in the area of sexuality. Today young people want to know the rules, but they won't find them in a newspaper's answer column, or in horoscopes, or in universities and schools. God's rules for sexuality are written in His guide book – the Bible.

God is not an oppressive joy-killer. The Bible says that God made some fences, and says: 'Within these fences you are free to do whatever you want. Enjoy the gift of sex. The fences keep you from wrecking your life. These are the rules to play by.'

If you live by God's rules and walk in the light you'll be a happy and free person. Jesus said: 'If the Son sets you free, you will be free indeed' (John 8:36). Free to serve the Lord, free to pray, free to worship without a guilty conscience and hypocritical smile. You are free with Jesus.

All of us are tempted, but temptation isn't sin. In the power of Jesus you can overcome temptation. The Bible says: 'I can do everything through Him who gives me strength' (Philippians 4:13). The Bible says: 'Sin shall not be your master, because you are not under the law, but under grace' (Romans 6:14).

The Bible says we are complete in Christ. When you open your heart to Him you are a total man or woman. But until you come to Christ your life is dead and you don't know it. Come to Christ. It's not too late.

6. JESUS CHRIST IS ALIVE AND RELEVANT FOR TODAY IN THE CALL OF ETERNITY

Is there life after death? Yes. What kind of life after death? The Bible says those who have Christ in their hearts go to heaven. We all dream about heaven, a perfect, marvellous place with no crying, disease or death. No more unhappiness. The Bible talks about being 'away from the body and at home with the Lord' (2 Corinthians 5:8). How exciting that is!

But unfortunately if you die without Christ you go to hell – the other place – the one we *don't* dream about. Hell is not a swear word, but an awful reality. And if you die without Christ, that's where you'll go, but not because God wants you there. The Bible clearly teaches that hell was prepared for the devil and his demons, not for people.

But if you hear God's voice and say: 'God, I don't care about You, or Your Son Jesus Christ, or Your Bible, or Your holiness. I am going to live my way' – then watch out. God says: 'There is a way that seems right to a man, but in the end it leads to death' (Proverbs 14:12).

But Jesus Christ said: 'I give them eternal life, and they shall never perish; no-one can snatch them out of my hand' (John 10:28). The Lord says: 'For God did not send his son into the world to condemn the world, but to save the world through him' (John 3:17).

The Bible says: 'The wages of sin is death, but the gift of God is eternal life in Christ Jesus our Lord' (Romans 6:23). It's a gift. You receive a gift by accepting it and saying: 'Thank you.' You can receive Christ the same way – by opening your heart to Him and saying: 'Thank You, God.'

You may be Catholic, Protestant, Muslim, Hindu, Buddhist, Jewish, or you may have no religion at all, but you want to know Jesus Christ. I want to introduce you to Christ, just as I would introduce you to any other friend.

You can receive Jesus Christ right now, but you must open the door of your heart by faith. The best way I know how to do it is by praying a simple prayer. I hope that you will open your heart to Christ right now.

Let's bow our heads and our hearts before God. I will lead you in a simple prayer, and by praying this prayer, you can open your heart to Jesus Christ right where you are:

Thank You, Heavenly Father, that Jesus Christ gives me eternal life. I don't deserve it, Lord. I deserve hell. I've broken Your laws and sinned against You. Thank You for the cross where Jesus died for me. I don't understand it all, but by faith, I believe in Jesus Christ. Lord, thank You for eternal life and for the cleansing of my sins because Christ now lives in me. I want to serve You, Lord Jesus. Bless my home, O Lord. Bless my loved ones. May they all serve You and live for Your glory. Bless England, O Lord. Bring revival to the land. And begin Your revival here in me. Thank You, Lord Jesus. I shall live for Your glory because Christ now lives in me. In His name I pray. Amen.

If you have just prayed this prayer and committed your life to Jesus Christ, or if you have any questions, please write to me at this address:

Luis Palau Evangelistic Team
European Division
175 Tower Bridge Road
London SE1 2AS
ENGLAND

BIBLIOGRAPHY

Adcock, E. F., *Charles H. Spurgeon: Prince of Preachers* (Gospel Trumpet Co., Anderson, Ind.), 1925

Brierley, Peter, *Mission to London Phase One: Who Responded?* (MARC Europe, London) 1984

Brierley, Peter, *Mission to London Phase Two: Who Went Forward?* (MARC Europe, London) 1985

Carey, S. Pearce, *William Carey* (Carey Press, London) 1934

Carwardine, Richard, *Trans-Atlantic Revivalism* (Greenwood) 1978

Fullerton, W. Y., *F. B. Meyer: A Biography* (Marshall, Morgan & Scott, London)

Harrison, Jan, *Attitudes to the Bible, God and the Church* (Bible Society London) 1983

High, Stanley, *Billy Graham* (McGraw-Hill, New York) 1956

Lewis, C. S., *The Four Loves* (Harcourt Brace, New York) 1960

Ninde, Edward S., *George Whitefield: Prophet-Preacher* (Abingdon, New York) 1924

Pollock, John, *Moody: The Biography* (Moody, Chicago) 1983

Railton, G. S., *The Authoritative Life of General William Booth: Founder of the Salvation Army* (Doran, New York) 1912

Sherwin, Oscar, *John Wesley, Friend of the People* (Twayne, New York) 1961

Smith, Gipsy Rodney, *Gipsy Smith, An Autobiography* (Revell) 1901

Smith, Oswald J., *Passion for Souls* (Marshall Morgan & Scott, London) 1965

Taylor, Dr and Mrs Howard, *Biography of James Hudson Taylor* (Hodder, London) 1973

Telford, John, *The Life of John Wesley* (Hunt & Eaton, New York) 1890

Wagner, D. M., *The Expository Method of G. Campbell Morgan* (Revell) 1957

Wayland, H. Lincoln (ed.), *Autobiography of George Mueller, the Life of Trust* (Baker, Grand Rapids) 1981

Whitefield, George, *Journals* (Banner of Truth Trust, Carlisle, Penn.) 1978

NOTES

PREFACE

1 *George Whitefield's Journals*, The Banner of Truth Trust, Carlisle, Penn., 1978.

CHAPTER 2

1 *World Evangelization News*, Lausanne Committee for World Evangelization, 11 October 1984.
2 Edward S. Ninde, *George Whitefield, Prophet-Preacher* (Abingdon Press, New York, 1924).
3 Oscar Sherwin, *John Wesley, Friend of the People* (Twayne Publishers, New York, 1961), p. 30.
4 John Telford, *The Life of John Wesley* (Hunt & Eaton, New York, 1890), pp. 114–15.
5 ibid., p. 157.
6 Sherwin, op. cit., p. 42.
7 *George Whitefield's Journals* (The Banner of Truth Trust, Carlisle, Pennsylvania, 1978), p. 323.
8 E. F. Adcock, *Charles H. Spurgeon: Prince of Preachers* (Gospel Trumpet Company, Anderson, Indiana, 1925), p. 57.
9 Luis Palau, 'Plan Great Plans', *Christian Herald*, 31 March 1984, p. 15.
10 John Pollock, *Moody: The Biography* (Moody Press, Chicago, 1983), p. 167.
11 ibid., p. 167.
12 ibid., p. 167.
13 'Mission accomplished, Billy Graham flies out . . . but he's back next year', *Church of England Newspaper*, 3 August 1984, p. 1.

14 'Let's face it: Join the crusade', *Birmingham Sunday Mercury*, 29 January 1984.
15 Billy Graham, personal letter to Luis Palau, Montreat, N. Carolina, 3 February 1984.

CHAPTER 4

1   C. S. Lewis, *The Four Loves* (Harcourt Brace, New York) 1960.
2   David Fletcher, 'One-parent child faces "grim time"', *Daily Telegraph*, June 1983.
3   Eddie Tait, 'Children and videos: the terrible proof', *Revival*, January 1984, p. 2.
4   Anthony Mascarenhas, 'Britain is "open house to heroin"', *Sunday Times*, 2 October 1983.
5   'Craze or crazy?' *Evangelism Today*, March 1984.
6   'You're so stuffy churches are told', *Baptist Times*, 21 July 1983, p. 5.
7   ibid., p. 5.
8   'Comment: What the bishop designate said', *Church of England Newspaper*, 25 May 1984, p. 4.
9   ibid., p. 4.
10 'By heresies distrest', *Economist*, 30 June 1984, p. 30.
11 Luis Palau, 'The fires of revival', *Christian Herald*, 17 March 1984, p. 10.

CHAPTER 5

1   *Let the Whole World Hear the Voice of God*, Luis Palau Evangelistic Team, 1983, p. 17.
2   Michael Botting, follow-up report of Luis Palau's 1982 Leeds crusade, Leeds, 17 December 1982.
3   Derek Williams, 'Thinking big about evangelism', *Crusade (Today)*, July 1981, p. 7.

CHAPTER 8

1   Roger Green, 'High hopes for evangelism', *Buzz*, May 1982, p. 31.

2 Armin Gesswein, 'It's time we woke up', *Revival*, June 1984, p. 3.
3 Oswald J. Smith, *Passion for Souls* (Marshall Morgan and Scott, London, 1965).
4 *World Evangelization News*, Lausanne Committee for World Evangelization, September–October 1983.
5 Brian Mills, 'Soaking England with prayer', *Revival*, June 1983, p. 12.

CHAPTER 10

1 Tom Davies, 'Hallelujah Inc.', *Sunday Express Magazine*, 24 June 1984, p. 17.
2 'Oofy Prosser's city column', *Punch*, 20 June 1984.
3 Frances Welch, 'A great crusade', *Acton Gazette and Post*, 21 June 1984, p. 15.
4 Graham Jones, 'I'm not crude, says soccer stadium evangelist', *Daily Telegraph*, 3 July 1984, p. 15.
5 Norman Lymberry, 'Food for thought', *Hemel Hempstead Gazette*, 27 July 1984.
6 Martyn Halsall, 'Challenge of the century', *Baptist Times*, 16 August 1984.
7 Martyn Halsall, 'High-scoring claims by football field evangelists', *Guardian*, 25 June 1984.
8 Garry Jenkins, 'Simple faith – or Almighty racket?' *Guardian*, 21 June 1984.
9 Veronica Horwell, 'The gift-wrapped Gospel according to Luis', *Sunday Times*, 3 June 1984. Copyright © Times Newspapers Ltd.
10 Gerard Noel, 'Heaven and hell', *Catholic Herald*, 15 June 1984.
11 'Comment: After Jenkins' consecration', *Church of England Newspaper*, 13 July 1984, p. 4.
12 John Cunningham, 'To pack the pews, first find your crusader', *Guardian*, 30 May 1984.
13 'Luis Palau on there being hell to pay', *Church of England Newspaper*, 13 January 1984.
14 William Marshall, 'God's mouthpiece', *Daily Mirror*, 30 June 1984, p. 15.
15 Richard Salvage, 'One way of preaching', *Ealing Gazette*, 18 May 1984.
16 'We'll feel the effects for years', *Baptist Times*, 21 June 1984, p. 1.

17 'Luis Palau's campaign to be extended', *Church Times*, 8 June 1984, p. 1.
18 Ray Hosking, 'Palau rekindles revival flames', *Impact*, Wesley Central Mission, Sydney, August 1984, p. 15.
19 Tom Davies, op. cit., p. 17.

CHAPTER 14

1 Anne Townsend, 'Luis Palau at Wembley', *Church of England Newspaper*, 28 October 1983, p. 1.
2 C. J. Cashmore, 'Changed by the Word', *Baptist Times*, 8 December 1983.

CHAPTER 15

1 Harvey Thomas, 'Don't ignore voices from the past', *Today*, June 1984, p. 4.

CHAPTER 17

1 'Mission to London is 155,000 pounds in red', *Church of England Newspaper*, 10 August 1984, p. 1.

CHAPTER 19

1 C. Peter Wagner, 'Plan Rosario: Milepost for Saturation Evangelism?' *Church Growth Bulletin*, September 1977, p. 147.
2 'Luis Palau's Mission to London: Million Pound Mission', *Today*, August 1983, p. 30.
3 'Comment: Crisis on our hands', *Church of England Newspaper*, 10 August 1984, p. 4.
4 Ian Coffey, 'Missions – where do we go from here?' *Today*, August 1984, p. 9.
5 Eric Delve, 'Mission to London – celebrate with confidence', *Idea*, Winter 1983/84, p. 6.
6 George Hider, 'Where were London's Christians?' *Church of England Newspaper*, 3 August 1984, p. 9.
7 Coffey, op. cit., p. 10.